We Need to Talk about Religious Education

of related interest

God-Curious
Exploring Eternal Questions
Stephen Cherry
ISBN 978 1 78592 199 5
eISBN 978 1 78450 473 1

Re-enchanting the Activist
Spirituality and Social Change
Keith Hebden
ISBN 978 1 78592 041 7
eISBN 978 1 78450 295 9

Children and Spirituality
Searching for Meaning and Connectedness
Brendan Hyde
ISBN 978 1 84310 589 3
eISBN 978 1 84642 754 1

The Spirit of the Child
Revised Edition
David Hay
ISBN 978 1 84310 371 4
eISBN 978 1 84642 473 1

Children's Perspectives on Believing and Belonging
Greg Smith
ISBN 978 1 90478 753 2
eISBN 978 1 90796 958 4

We Need to Talk about Religious Education

Manifestos for the Future of RE

Edited by
Mike Castelli
Mark Chater

Foreword by
Professor Linda Woodhead, MBE

Jessica Kingsley *Publishers*
London and Philadelphia

First published in 2018
by Jessica Kingsley Publishers
73 Collier Street
London N1 9BE, UK
and
400 Market Street, Suite 400
Philadelphia, PA 19106, USA

www.jkp.com

Library of Congress Cataloging in Publication Data
Names: Mike Castelli, editor.
Title: We need to talk about RE : manifestos for the future of religious education
/ edited by Mike Castelli and Mark Chater.
Other titles: We need to talk about Religious Education
Description: Philadelphia : Jessica Kingsley Publishers, 2017. | Includes index.
Identifiers: LCCN 2017022503 | ISBN 9781785922695
Subjects: LCSH: Religious education--Great Britain.
Classification: LCC BL42.5.G7 W4 2017 | DDC 200.71/041--dc23 LC record
available at https://lccn.loc.gov/2017022503

British Library Cataloguing in Publication Data
A CIP catalogue record for this book is available from the British Library

ISBN 978 1 78592 269 5
eISBN 978 1 78450 565 3

Printed and bound in the United States

CONTENTS

PART 2: FUTURES

FOREWORD

PROFESSOR LINDA WOODHEAD, MBE

Modern Britain – and England in particular – is careless with its culture. I don't mean the arts; I mean the frameworks for living that we inherit, adapt and pass on – our 'software'. Perhaps that is because culture, like language, is so constitutive of who we are that we don't often stop to think about it. Or perhaps it is because we have become more complacent about culture than about politics and the economy.

Whatever the reason, the study of our own culture or cultures is so neglected in universities that it often falls to scholars of religion to describe what is happening. A number of us have been in the forefront of charting the immense changes that have taken place since the 1980s and are still ongoing: the growth of significant religious diversity and, even more importantly, the shift from being a nation where a majority of people describe themselves as 'Christian' to one in which they say they have 'no religion' (e.g. Woodhead 2016).

The travails and difficulties in becoming 'multi-cultural' and 'multi-faith' are always in the news. What is less appreciated is how quickly and, on the whole, successfully Britain has adapted. I believe that RE teachers in schools deserve a good deal of credit. Children are on the frontline of cultural change, and this means that since the 1960s RE teachers have been as well. On the whole they adapted with immense skill and sensitivity. Supported by Standing Advisory Councils on RE, local education authorities and local Subject Advisors, they ensured that the transition from Christian Instruction to Religious Studies took place efficiently and effectively. Some academics like my predecessor at Lancaster University, Ninian Smart, played a role as well.

RE's success, however, occurred largely in spite of the legislative frameworks and resourcing it received from central government, and in the absence of any serious and sustained attempt in England and Wales to address the role of RE in a changing context. The current settlement for RE is virtually unchanged since the Education Act of 1944 – the only subject area that finds itself in this unenviable position. There have been no changes at all to the basic requirements concerning religion in schools, which still include a daily act of collective worship of a broadly Christian character, the right to withdraw from RE lessons, and local determination of RE syllabuses – precluding a national syllabus for the subject. All of this harks back to an era that no longer exists, and puts the subject on a less stable footing than all other subjects.

It's no wonder that RE is struggling. As if these disabilities were not enough, the recent withering of local authorities under the pressure of academisation, combined with under-resourcing of the subject, has made the situation even worse. It simply cannot continue like this – the infrastructure on which it all depended has virtually disappeared.

It was concern about this situation that led Charles Clarke and me to publish a pamphlet called *A New Settlement: Religion in Schools* (Clarke and Woodhead 2015). Charles had become aware of the problems facing RE when he was Education Secretary, and had started to initiate reform, hoping – in vain – that the process would continue once he had left office. I too had become aware of the importance of the topic from my own research and that of others, from publicly available data on schools, and from expert testimony interrogated through the Westminster Faith Debates or private consultations. We show how RE has suffered over many years from a kind of exceptionalism, born of outdated assumptions and structures, which has isolated it and inhibited reform. RE has been freighted with too little significance and too much.

Since publication we have continued to speak to experts and to carry out research, with the intention of publishing a revised version and set of recommendations in due course. We are learning all the time, not least from the remarkable professional community that is also fighting for the subject. We are just a small part of a much wider movement of concern that is stimulating informed debate about what needs to change. This book is an important contribution to this enterprise.

Having no religious affiliation is now the new norm in Britain, more so for every generation under forty. Research is revealing the profile of the new no-religion majority: prizing freedom and tolerance, typically more liberal in matters of morality than most religious people or the population as a whole, open to religious and spiritual practices, and firmly disinclined to join religious groups or adopt labels, they enjoy their contact with religious and cultural diversity but have little respect for or trust in major religious leaders (Woodhead 2016). I do not believe that this state of affairs presages the disappearance of organised religion: religion itself is changing in the UK, hardening to narrow stances in some places and softening in others, and it remains institutionally embedded, not least in faith schools.

A globalised world, digitally rich schools and families, continuing migration and social mobility have brought current generations into increasing contact with ethical, religious and cultural diversity. The fallout in liberal democracies is that prescriptive ethical systems and moral paternalism, exclusive truth claims, dogmatic teachings and narratives of cultural or spiritual superiority are rapidly becoming less believable and attractive to the majority. Compounding this, the failure of some religious groups to admit to their own internal diversity or to engage people with the spiritual in ways which are meaningful to them has resulted in their being stranded as the tide of an unselfconsciously sceptical majority sweeps by them.

In such a context, and faced by such a cultural sea-change, the provision for RE in our schools needs urgent attention and reform. As more people in this country lose contact with religion but religion's global impact continues to be profound, RE's importance remains undiminished.

However heroic the efforts of individual teachers, the obstacles facing them are now too great to be overcome. With some notable exceptions, the quality of RE in schools in recent decades has been found to be deficient. Too many schools have given up teaching the subject at all, despite the legal requirement to do so, and RE is more likely than other subjects to be taught by unqualified teachers. Many of its professional assumptions and nearly all of its legal and administrative machinery reflect a religious and cultural Britain of yesteryear.

That RE is languishing in this decaying state is truly shocking.

From this situation, the new RE that must be born will draw on the advances still being made by teachers and educationalists struggling against the tide, a number of whom make contributions to this excellent collection. I welcome *We Need to Talk about Religious Education* as a significant, thoughtful and constructive compilation of contributions to an increasingly pressing debate about the subject's future in UK schools. It reflects a diversity of approaches and joins a growing list of publications and initiatives calling for change, presaging the possibilities of a new era for RE in schools.

Professor Linda Woodhead, MBE, University of Lancaster

References

Clarke, C. and Woodhead, L. (2015) *A New Settlement: Religion and Belief in Schools*. Lancaster University: Westminster Faith Debates. Accessed on 25 May 2017 at http://faithdebates.org.uk/wp-content/uploads/2015/06/A-New-Settlement-for-Religion-and-Belief-in-schools.pdf

Woodhead, L. (2016) 'The rise of "No Religion" in Britain: The emergence of a new cultural majority.' *Journal of the British Academy 4*, 245–261.

EDITORS' INTRODUCTION

We Need to Talk about Religious Education is a multiple manifesto for a much-needed, little-understood subject in the school curriculum. This book gives a voice to sixteen emerging and established leaders in the theory and practice of religious education. The book's title is deliberately pluralistic, indicating not only the authors' desire to discuss and develop their ideas in dialogue with the readers, but also a perception that the wider public – parents, teachers, school leaders, academics, faith leaders and other community stakeholders – need to discuss RE and find a new, assured place for it, based on a shared understanding of the common good. There are many reasons why we need to talk about RE:

- Schools, led by middle and senior leaders with passion and energy for improving the prospects of young people, are moving away from compliance culture and innovating in curriculum and pedagogy; they are also faced with exceptionally hard spending curbs and the painful decisions that must follow. We need to talk about RE to ensure its place in this changing school curriculum.

- Teachers of RE, whose voices are seldom heard beyond social media, are cultural and religious heroes caught up in a conflicted education system, energetically offering wisdom to young minds, trying to protect themselves and each other while the educational pillars fall around them. We need to talk about approaches to RE that are relevant and supportive to teachers and pupils in this conflicted education system.

- The RE experiment in the UK is unique, and has much to offer the wider world, but is in danger of isolation, neglect and dismemberment at a time of unprecedented religious, cultural and political tension. We need to talk about how RE recognises and faces such tensions.

- Leaders of the RE community, whether professional teachers, representatives of belief communities, or both, struggle to create a clear and safe positioning for RE between the wreckage of old assumptions and structures and the messy, incomplete birth of the new. We need to talk about RE to find some consensus in this positioning of the subject so that we articulate a coherent case for RE's relevance at a time of social and political change.

- Civic society and members of belief communities are seeking an imaginative civics that will facilitate living with otherness, bringing comfort and reassurance to those whose identities feel threatened, without retreating into nativist or fundamentalist paradigms. We need to talk about RE and its contribution to such an imaginative civics.

The voices that talk about RE in this book are diverse, polemical, future-facing and informed by theory and practice. They have much to say about RE's journey, the places it has come from and its possible future development in these changeable times. They are voices of experience and of fresh insight, of radical reform and of gradualist evolution. By and large they are not defenders of the status quo in RE: such voices are hard to find right now.

Yet the 'we' who need to speak about RE are many more than the authors in this book. We as a teaching profession need a continuing conversation about RE and its relationship to wider learning. We as a nation need a conversation about public religious literacy and its relationship to other forms of literacy. The need for religious literacy among people of all ages was stressed by the Archbishop of Canterbury in the wake of the London Bridge terrorist attack of June 2017. A lack of basic understanding of doctrines, he argued, could lead to poor empathy with others and a weak grasp of one's own religion. He added that Christianity and every religion contained both 'heroism and beauty' and also a 'dark side', and implied that religious literacy should include the capacity to distinguish the one from the other (Welby 2017). Finally, we – globally, as neighbours – need to be in dialogue about religion and belief; we need an open discussion about what we have a right and duty to teach our children.

Talking about RE must also lead somewhere. Nearly all the contributors here are arguing for a change of direction in RE. The directions indicated in these manifestos are many, varied, informed by experience and, we hope, exciting. This is not a programmatic work in the sense of building and advocating a single diagnosis and treatment for RE. It is, we hope, a provocation to our colleagues and political leaders, and the wider public, demonstrating a will to listen, sharing work that is still fluid and in development, and pointing to change with integrity.

Mike Castelli and Mark Chater

Reference

Welby, J. (2017, 5 June) 'London attack: Archbishop Justin Welby warns against "religious illiteracy".' BBC News. Accessed on 25 June 2017 at www.bbc.co.uk/news/av/uk-politics-40156995/london-attack-archbishop-justin-welby-warns-against-religious-illiteracy

Part 1

CONTEXT

INTRODUCTION

Waking to the European Union referendum result on the morning of 24 June 2016, and in the days and months that followed, was a crash course in change. The cultural commentator and leadership philosopher Charles Handy, writing nearly 30 years ago, described two kinds of change: continuous and discontinuous. Agreeing that continuous, gradual evolution is more comfortable, Handy also acknowledged that discontinuous change was often more productive and life-giving, even when destructive:

> Do we always need a painful jolt to start re-thinking? ... Did the Challenger shuttle have to explode before NASA reorganised its decision-making systems and priorities?' (Handy 1989, p.9)

Handy suggested that discontinuous change happens in societies that are 'tramlined' (p.7) and unable to grow by questioning their cherished assumptions.

The UK is now in a turbulent period of discontinuous change, bringing disruption to cultural, political and communal life, to our assumptions about ourselves as a nation, about each other and our place in the world. This cannot fail to affect our education system, belief communities, teachers and pupils. RE and education are no strangers to change. The question is what we do about it.

In a recently published retrospective on RE policy making, Barbara Wintersgill and Alan Brine, both former Her Majesty's Inspectors (HMIs) of RE nationally in England, warn that RE is uniquely vulnerable in this time of change. Arguing that

RE had a 'golden age' between 1993 and 2010, characterised by national development in a partnership between local and national bodies (Wintersgill and Brine 2016, p.264), they lament that RE's underlying weaknesses, such as confusion of purpose and statutory oddness, were not resolved in those good years. RE's national 'life support' (p.272) enabled local institutions to continue their work, but was abruptly switched off in 2010, when the curriculum agency was abolished and key guidance documents on RE were pulled down from websites. This was followed in 2013 by the last of the Ofsted national surveys that had done so much to illumine the state of RE. While RE cannot be said to have returned to its vulnerable status pre-1988, it faces a lonely future unless key change processes are accepted and sponsored by central government. 'Many RE teachers, lecturers and consultants fear that the changes in education and the loss of government support…have left RE irrevocably weakened' (p.275).

There is, however, a vital distinction between facing up to these difficulties and being crushed by them. The contributors in this first section, though they offer divergent solutions, are united in the boldness with which they recognise the challenges and call for new thinking or new structures. Each of them may be said to offer the 'painful jolt' prescribed by Handy, to encourage the RE community to re-think its context and shape its future.

In this first part, Clive Lawton shares a personal take on the subject's failure to keep pace historically, and suggests three significant cultural and structural changes, long overdue, that could transform RE's credibility and integrity. Peter Schreiner places RE in the wider European context in which economic and instrumentalist priorities have not been sufficiently questioned even when they create a hostile environment for RE in its many forms. Richard Kueh argues that RE's vulnerabilities are not all external, and that the subject's failure to define a powerful knowledge-base clearly constitutes its greatest weakness both pedagogically and in terms of credibility. Mark Chater focuses on the legal arrangements and structures for RE in England, demonstrating how they impact directly on poor standards in RE and how they could be changed without alienating RE's key stakeholders. Andrew Lewis contributes an account of how Catholic RE in England has evolved distinctively, its points of comparison with wider RE models in community schools revealing some similarities, shared concerns and debates, and differences based on principle. Gillian Georgiou and Kathryn Wright, facing the identity challenge in RE, advocate a three-way balance between theology, philosophy and social sciences, and offer primary and secondary examples of each. Sushma Sahajpal, drawing on her reflections as a consultant, envisions a new core integrity for our subject, one based on the child's right to a cultural identity that is educated and open to diversity.

RE's uncertain context has to be understood before we move forward into new principles and practice. Perhaps because of our 'liminality' (Conroy *et al.* 2013, p.35), our existence in a sort of epistemic and pedagogical twilight zone, we have to work harder than some other subjects in order to reach educational clarity and security. Each of these contributions begins by recognising RE's fragile and contested nature, and suggests a journey from there.

References

Conroy, J., Lundie, D., Davis, R., Baumfield, V. *et al.* (2013). *Does Religious Education Work?* London: Bloomsbury.

Handy, C. (1989) *The Age of Unreason.* London: Arrow Books.

Wintersgill, B. and Brine, A. (2016) 'Government National Agencies for Inspection and Curriculum Development in RE.' In B. Gates (ed.) *Religion and Nationhood: Insider and Outsider Perspectives on Religious Education in England* (pp.255–279). Tübingen: Mohr Siebeck.

Chapter 1

TIME TO ABANDON RELIGIOUS EDUCATION

*Ditching an Out-of-Date Solution
to an Out-of-Date Problem*

CLIVE A. LAWTON

It is time to abandon RE as we have known it. The practice of the subject in England has far outgrown its legal, nominal and religious skin. Religious and secular worldviews, and the identities that surround them, remain a crucial form of study. But, as I shall show through a brief personal journey through the historical development of RE, the proper study of these aspects of the world is now held back. The factors holding it back include a confused sense of the country's identity, culture and history, a fatal conflation of RE with collective worship, and an excessive level of expectation placed on the subject. Three key features of current RE are discussed, found wanting and earmarked for abandonment: the religious exceptionalism that permits faith representatives to have a part in writing syllabuses, the parental right to withdraw their child from RE, and the expectation of 'learning from' as a specific attainment outcome.

RE and the modern world

No sensible person can now argue that religion is not a central feature of human life and motivation across the planet. That being the self-evident case, it would be a gross dereliction to leave children unable to manage its clearly compelling power.

Young people need to be taught to cope with the delirious and dangerous, uplifting, enlightening, beautiful and seductive power and inescapability of messages and inducements to engage with sex and drugs. Religion is no different, for good or for ill. Governments throughout the world are seeking ways to prevent young people from engaging with destructive religious doctrines but do not seem to understand that to deal with the phenomenon of religious extremism, one will have to teach much more confidently about religion overall.

It is frankly embarrassing to hear politicians of every stripe say from time to time that this or that atrocity is a gross perversion of this or that religion, since whichever religion it is is a religion of peace. A brief spell in a proper Religious Studies class would reveal something more complex: for example, that certain Christians found nothing inconsistent with their beliefs in slogging it out in Northern Ireland or on the Serbian/Croatian border; that certain Muslims feel impelled by their readings of Islam to fight against apostasy or idolatry; that certain Jews cannot find it conscionable to move out of the ancient heartlands of biblical Israel in the West Bank, whatever conflict this might provoke; that there are militant Buddhists in Sri Lanka, Hindus prepared to blow up mosques in India, and Sikhs who in no way condemn the assassination of Indira Gandhi by her Sikh bodyguard. Any child educated as I would hope would look at such political 'leaders' with incredulity, wondering how they could utter such specious nonsense without even the basic knowledge required of one of the most motivating forces of the 21st century.

How did we get here?

My parents, being practising and committed Jews, took necessary advantage of the 1944 legislation to 'withdraw' me from RE and 'Assembly'. Like just about every other Jew of my age, withdrawn or not, standing outside non-soundproofed school halls, we can all run off the Lord's Prayer with the best of them and go soggy with nostalgia at Christmas carols. In those days, primary schools up and down the country would engage in creating table centre-pieces, Christmas cards and decorations for about three months. Many of us sang carols along with the school choir. We developed highly sophisticated instant editorial capacities, dropping key words as we sang, thereby keeping ourselves pure from Christological taint.

This post-1944 RE was an odd thing. Born of a compromise between the Church and the State, local authority schools were all required to *teach* Christianity, but shorn of any of its denominational specificities, and no one was required to *learn* it. This arrangement necessarily taught the meta-lesson, so widely absorbed by British society, that religion mattered but not to the extent that it might affect anyone. Indeed it might possibly be true that the vast majority of the people who took religion really seriously were those who somehow excluded themselves from RE, either by withdrawing into separate schools – Catholics, Church of England voluntary-aided schools and a small sprinkling of Jews and others – or withdrawing their children from classes because they did not agree with what they imagined would be taught there. How odd that those who withdrew their children from RE might have been the only ones to really believe in its possibilities and potency.

But in fact, the subject had been entirely emasculated. By requiring that the religion (Christianity) taught should have no features of the universal reality of religion – that it is a lived thing or it is nothing – teachers were reduced to a menu of Bible stories, moral exhortations and, in latter days, topical discussion with an ethical tinge.

By the late 1960s, a few teachers and thinkers had realised that RE needed to get to grips with the growing reality that religion in the UK was not only Christianity. (Jews had been present in Britain for 250 years perfectly visibly, but they did not really count for these purposes, having long been tolerated as sort of proto-Christians.) These '60s pioneers tried to develop the subject in a different direction informed by phenomenology (Smart 1968).

With the help of scholars such as the Shap Working Party on World Religions in Education, teaching about world religions became accepted curriculum policy (Schools Council 1971).

The climate of the times gave teachers the licence to teach about religions in their variety, thus seeking to ensure that children might learn from such studies in any way that might seem relevant to them. By the late 1970s, several Agreed Syllabuses had explicitly required the teaching of several religions and were hoping that RE teachers would be equal to the challenge (Copley 2008). (Given that most teachers of RE were hardly equipped to teach Christianity, let alone any other religion, this hope was not quite as quixotic as it might have seemed.)

But this attempt to make RE relevant to the world in which children actually lived eventually came to grief. In the great curriculum wars of the late 1980s, the proposal to create a National Curriculum, despite its avowed intention of creating a curriculum fit for the modern age, found that the key battle-grounds were not Science or Technology or Maths, but Literature, History and, of course, Religion. The fight was on for the soul of the nation. In the end, as we now all know, the 1944 fudge was perpetuated, but with the valuable addition that children must now also be taught about non-Christian religions too.

The positions taken by legislators in the debates on the 1988 Act reflect a kaleidoscope of religious perspectives. Perhaps some of them knew that school RE had contributed not a little to the precipitous decline in church attendance. Conversely, the then Chief Rabbi, the late Lord Jakobovits, sitting in the House of Lords, argued vehemently with me that such special attention was a good thing since it would help to ensure that, on the one hand, Britain remained a country with religious sensibilities at its heart; and, on the other hand, that Jews would be clear that the core of British life was not conducive to Jewish religious interests and so Jews would seek out more specific Jewish teaching. *Hansard* (1988) tells it clearly. The then Bishop of London spoke in favour of a mixed religious education through the local Agreed Syllabus system, while the then Chief Rabbi spoke up for community, culture, family and the past. In the event, the old protections were preserved. The subject had to be taught, but it did not have to be learned. Withdrawal survived. RE was not for everyone: the view that it was potentially a threatening evangelical activity was respected in law.

Indeed, Lord Jakobovits spoke up for the need for specifically Christian education as a necessary bulwark against an increasingly materialist and 'pagan' society. Others contributing to the debate slipped and slid between arguing that Christianity should be especially prominent in the subject matter and arguing that children needed to receive a Christian education. Small wonder then that the right to withdraw was felt necessary to protect children from being unfairly evangelised, sitting at their state school classroom desks. In vain did others point out that such confessional work was no part of non-religious maintained schools.

But the forces of progressive attempts to broaden the base of RE were not yet defeated. Much debate was had about what constituted the size or scale of the Christian component in RE, given that it must be in the majority. Should it be more than 50 percent or just the biggest bit, or could you count 'moral' discussions as part of the Christian component?

RE and collective worship

Even more problematic was the preservation of the collective act of worship, which was embarrassing more and more schools across the country. Headteachers did not feel equipped or committed to leading such things; RE teachers did not necessarily want their subject to be dragged into explicitly religious performance; and there were a host of other problems and issues. By the early 1990s, collective worship had frequently become almost Buddhist, with moments of reflection or simply opportunities for someone to read an uplifting story of human endeavour.

The untenability of the situation (which still now pertains, on paper) was exposed and accentuated by the bizarre circular issued by the Department for Education (DfE 1994). To the best of my knowledge, for the first time ever, a government department was defining what were the essential features of Christianity. This circular may well be the only departmental document ever to be produced by civil servants unashamedly using Christian confessional language, despite any attempts at moderation by the Church of England and other concerned parties. A government circular referring to 'The Lord Krishna' or the 'Prophet Muhammad PBUH' would probably raise eyebrows. But demanding that, to be Christian, collective worship must ascribe special status to Jesus Christ demonstrated that even the mandarins of the DfE might have benefited from a good dose of proper Religious Studies.

Our expectations from RE

Over the last nearly 30 years since the creation of the National Curriculum, various attempts have been made to broaden, loosen, enrich and diversify the compulsory curriculum or the Basic Curriculum, i.e. the National Curriculum plus RE and sex education. Many suspect that the creation of this concept of the Basic Curriculum arose because the civil servants had originally forgotten about RE, or did not know where to put it exactly. From the outset, there was a dim recognition that schooling should in some way relate to life (not just subjects and academic achievement), and a range of required fields were to be crammed in one way or another: economic education, keyboard skills, environmental education, citizenship, health education, careers education and so on. In amongst this lurked spiritual, moral, social and cultural development, supposedly an aim of education as a whole (DfE 2013), with the additional load that schools were actually expected to deliver on this front in such a manner that they could be judged by Ofsted.

A key aspect of cultural development related not least to Christianity as one of the bedrocks of British culture. A decently educated child from our schools should have a clue as to why a cathedral looked the way it did, what Milton was talking about and why Guy Fawkes and friends may have tried to blow up James I and his parliament. In an attempt to justify the continued inclusion of RE in the curriculum in the face of increasingly vociferous challenge from secularists (Jackson and O'Grady 2007), the perfectly reasonable argument was posited that young people need to know about Christianity in order to understand British life and British values. Indeed, the logic of such a position could well lead one to the conclusion that the pupils who might most need to study RE for these reasons would be those from non-Christian backgrounds most of all. Yet one might easily argue very similarly in relation to Islam in particular: how can a person understand the dynamics of so many contemporary public debates, social diversity, xenophobic conflict, terrorist activity and cultural dispute, without knowing something of the true realities of Islam, its sense of self, its history, its aspirations and its diverse manifestations?

But the continued right of withdrawal gives the lie to this, or at least exposes the contradiction and confusion right at the heart of the understanding and aspirations for the subject called RE.

Furthermore, current arrangements militate against increasing the number of properly trained RE teachers being employed. There is anyway a shortage of such teachers; but this shortage is aggravated by RE rarely counting towards a school's profile, league table position and other significant measures of quality. If a Head can cover the compulsory provision of RE by relying in large part on those who have a 'feel' for religion, or who occasionally go to church, why would they not? It is to the great credit of so many schools that this does not happen everywhere. But such perverse incentives prevent the subject from being wholly professional, and make it liable to stray into confessional expression, even unwittingly. For example, I remember the genuine sympathy that my teachers demonstrated for me being deprived of Christmas, with not a flicker of awareness that I had a pretty good festival most months, not to mention Shabbat every week. Such unintended, unexamined cultural myopia does not win confidence amongst minority communities and dissenting groups.

So RE now is popularly expected to be the main locus for moral development, a key locus for cultural development, an environment for developing spiritual awareness and sensitivity and, along the way, garnering a coherent grasp of half a dozen or more religious traditions. All this in often only one lesson a week, not infrequently with a teacher whose first specialism is other than RE. Is it reasonable to expect any of this, let alone all of it? And yet this 21st-century education system at least tolerates it, and apparently requires it.

A consideration of the poor thinking behind just three aspects of these expectations – the Agreed Syllabus system, the withdrawal clause and 'learning from' – exposes how threadbare and devoid of coherence the subject now is.

The Agreed Syllabus system

The arrangement for the production of an Agreed Syllabus, local authority by local authority, is a wonderful thing. No other subject requires a wide range of stakeholders to come together and decide the purpose and aims of the subject, and what exactly is to be taught. Not only are Agreed Syllabus conferences apparently almost designed to fail; they actually give cause for faith in miracles on a regular basis, because they instead frequently produce impressively thoughtful and significant proposals. Wondrous though this process is, it throws up again the anomalous nature of the subject and the exceptionalism accorded to RE and to religious communities. Such special arrangements do not enhance the status of the subject; rather they diminish it. Nevertheless, despite the leeway given to local authorities to make up their own minds as to what to cover and how, certain areas of consensus have emerged.

The prime half-dozen of religions to be studied is widely accepted in RE circles. But why should pupils learn about these in particular? Is it because they are significant in the study or history of religious traditions? Or their numerical or historical significance in the history of the UK? Or their current impact on British society, or world realities? Or because of their oddness, or typicality, or innocuousness, or controversy? Where do other philosophical traditions like Humanism fit in? Humanism and non-religious spiritualities play an increasingly large part in the nation's beliefs, especially the young (Heelas 2005; Heelas and Woodhead 2000). What place is there for other religions and ancient and widely recognised traditions such as Confucianism, Taoism or the Bahá'í faith? These traditions, and others, play a part in the lives of some children in this country. Yet their appearance in syllabuses is haphazard, sometimes making it into the curriculum because of some local demographic quirk.

These questions were pertinent 40 to 50 years ago. They are pressing now. More and more has been loaded on to the subject without any concomitant consideration of how to do it with the resources and status available. Assuming the government has no intention of actually resourcing the subject any more generously than it does at the moment, and no one has the influence to upgrade its status, then it seems essential that the subject must undergo root-and-branch review: it must change to deliver on the things we actually urgently need to be well done in our schools, for the benefit of the emerging 21st-century citizens we hope for.

Providing what is reasonable and desirable: An end to the right to withdraw

Despite some of the more lurid reactions to the Brexit vote, pretty well everyone knows that we will still live in a fairly globalised and mobile world. Many of our youngsters will live parts of their lives abroad, or live amongst foreigners in the UK. The passions and concerns of others will impact on our lives no less and probably even more than they do now.

Given this flexing of British life and realities, it becomes even more urgent to secure a strong understanding of the underpinnings of British culture and society while being confident enough to avoid feeling threatened or challenged when faced with a view that is not felt to be native. The trick then is to square the circle between a diverse, globalised world and a desire to promote 'British values'.

Exploring a diversity of truth claims, widely held and often mutually exclusive, seems like a really worthwhile way for today's children to spend some of their time in school. The same is true for claims and approaches to the good life. Actually to have a slot in the timetable and curriculum when this can be done is a valuable legacy not to be squandered. Taught well, young people could use such time to consider diverse approaches, learn how to accommodate attitudes with which they do not agree, and indeed debate when a line should be drawn beyond which accommodation would be a step too far. They could cultivate curiosity and openness together with a firm grasp of why the British cultural landscape is as it is. Many adult Jews, Muslims, Hindus and Humanists of my acquaintance will tell you how many assumptions and norms are still dependent on unexamined Christian legacies.

Why anyone would want to withdraw their child from such an education should demand rigorous examination. Since the development of such attitudes and knowledge is essential to the good functioning of UK society now and in future, any desire to withdraw children should be strongly resisted. But in order to do so, the subject would have to change almost beyond recognition.

Under a reformed RE, the right of withdrawal should be withdrawn. Parents have no right to prevent their children from understanding the world in which they live and into which they will grow. We do not allow parents to withdraw their children from geography in the fear they might become Brazilian, even though they may so love what they learn about Brazil that they resolve to live there; so nor should we legitimise the fear that in RE, as rewritten, a child might somehow become something 'other'. If that child ever does get to Brazil, their RE will have equipped them not to be surprised at the strange amalgam of Roman Catholicism and animism that will slowly unfold before their eyes. They would be seriously under-educated if they felt that simply knowing that most Brazilians are 'Christian' would see them through. Though this analogy might seem absurd, I use it to demonstrate the strangeness of the fear of well-taught RE, and the vast gulf between it and confessional religious education or instruction. Furthermore, even that fear appears misplaced; there is no evidence I know of that any pupil has been induced to adopt a religion as a result of RE in school.

Of course, we must accept that allowing young people to think for themselves might well result in them changing their own position or simply developing a certain scepticism towards that which they have been baldly told to accept. If parents wish to resist that for their children, they would be wise to educate them in an environment that might help them avoid the proper atmosphere of open enquiry. This form of education, if it can be so called, should not be at the state's expense. (This is not an opposition to denominational state schools, provided they offer at least a limited course of RS along with their confessional programmes. In voluntary-aided schools, for example, the confessional programmes and a proportion of main school funding is properly paid for by the community sponsoring the school, in recognition of the fact that it is not for the state to promote any particular religion.)

'Learning from': An anachronism

In the new dispensation, pupils would learn *about* religion and belief, but what about learning *from* religion? This two-pronged mantra became increasingly accepted as a definition of the attainment targets of the subject ever since real efforts were made to professionalise it. The mantra helped to finesse fears that RE was becoming 'merely academic' and losing any personal relevance.

Clearly it is no part of a state 'secular' school's remit to help pupils find their own religion. The state has no appropriate role in religious formation, or in the facilitation of young people being influenced by religion. Nor is it the function of such a school to undermine the family's religion of the home. But any sincere study of religion as it is lived and understood will provide both inspiring and dispiriting examples of what religion can do in people's lives. Exploration and consideration of such stories and events are indubitably part of the subject. Every subject teacher, perhaps especially in the Humanities, hopes that the material studied will enlarge pupils' insights, through a greater capacity to understand and engage constructively with the world. Thus pupils will develop the tools and skills for thinking about religion – and its sister, non-religion – intelligently and respectfully.

Respect, of course, is not a synonym for the toleration of everything. Pupils will no doubt grow in their convictions as to what lies beyond the pale for them. But they will do so in an informed and thoughtful way. Vituperation about this or that unfamiliar practice, and labelling new religions as cults or commitment as extremism, will hopefully be challenged in the RS classroom, demanding of pupils that their judgements are based on more thoughtful and consequential grounds than those often displayed by tabloid headlines and social media trolls.

With such a subject, pupils might be equipped to consider the extent to which al-Qaeda is articulating a valid approach to Islam, how it is possible to have militant Buddhists in Sri Lanka, on what basis some leaders of the worldwide Anglican Church can oppose the consecration of female or gay bishops, whether or not Israeli settlers in Hebron are using their religion for political ambitions, how a few 'pro-life' Christians can justify harming or even killing doctors who perform abortions, and whether or not the vehement atheists of the modern age understand religion.

Such children too will not be shocked to discover how many other children do not celebrate Christmas in the UK, and that they do not feel any loss as a result. Similarly, those children who do not celebrate Christmas will not feel that the widespread marking of the event is designed to undermine them or leave them out, understanding as they will the history and culture of these isles for more than a millennium.

No doubt such study will lead the more thoughtful ones to wonder whether or not religion might have a part in their lives. They will earn a healthy capacity to recognise and resist attempts to persuade from the more proselytising traditions, and also to understand why other religions do not make the same attempts.

Such children will emerge better equipped to understand the Christian underpinnings of British culture – literature, architecture, cuisine, calendar, language, music, art – as rich cultural capital, not givens. They will make a reasonable stab at differentiating between legitimate and illegitimate articulations of religion and philosophy. They will show an open-hearted interest in ways of life not their own. Above all, they will have an acceptance that the way we do things here is not the only valid way.

But no more fudge. 'Learning from' is an obsolete leftover from a bygone age – the middle of the last century. In the new RE, children will not be expected to 'learn from' religion as if it has a special right to call on children to see the world from its particular point of view. In a diverse modern society, oddly both more secular and more religious than in the last century (Heelas and Woodhead 2000), religion's special right to influence should no longer be smuggled into the curriculum. At the same time, nothing should be done in the RE classroom to prevent children from learning from the study of religions and religion.

Conclusion: Beyond RE

So what to do? The subject as it is cannot survive in its present form. Called 'RE' but strangely transmuting into 'RS' as soon as any examination looms, surrounded by fears that it is really only 'RI' from which dissenters and bigots might need protection, the subject is now exposed as being a huge over-filled bucket built on too many fault lines. (The mixed metaphors are deliberate to accentuate the clumsy absurdity of what now pertains.) But this does not imply that we must evacuate the field; rather, we need only clear the ground so that good things can grow healthily.

I propose that the subject be renamed 'Religious Studies' ('RS'), because that has academic validity and should be the core of what goes on in these lessons. Children should learn about religions and religion, and also consider non-religious approaches and philosophies. Over time, they should develop a rich insight into the variety of religions and philosophies, cultivating a capacity to question intelligently but respectfully, and developing empathetic skills in recognising how religion plays the part in adherents' lives that all human beings find in something or other. Religion is not just 'faith', as the (Protestant?) English synonym has it, but also community, tradition and culture, clustered around certain theological and philosophical assertions.

In this, it matters not that this or that religious tradition has been covered, but that the pupil is prepared for a possible eventual encounter with an adherent. Armed with the right attitude, the skill to question and some vantage point to make sense of the answers, such a pupil will be well set up to cope with religion in the 21st century.

In this new field, a pupil will no longer be baffled by popes, archbishops, cathedrals and Quakers. Religion will be studied as the social phenomenon it is. The rich roots and underpinnings that Christianity has provided for so much of British society will make more sense.

This field does not call merely for some kind of detached anthropology, a condescending archaeology, a bloodless phenomenology, or simply cool analysis and description. Religions and worldviews are contemporary, motivating and hugely consequential. Leaving young people unable to understand their diverse essence, and how and why they work for at least half the world's population, would be a dreadful dereliction of a modern education. The subject should not be dry or simply factual. Along with cognitive weight, it needs emotional heft and warm engagement, otherwise the topic will be sold short. But after all, any enthusiastic teacher of any subject will help their pupils to learn to use the perspective or their subject as a tool to resist and critique superficial and spurious viewpoints. This is true of the sciences, arts, maths and languages.

Finally, what about 'moral development'? That is the business of every teacher. If not, we're all doomed, and RE – or RS – won't save us.

References

Copley, T. (2008) *Teaching Religion: Sixty Years of Religious Education in England and Wales*. Exeter: University of Exeter Press.

Department for Education (1994) *Collective Worship in Schools* (Circular 1/94). London: DfE. Accessed on 24 May 2017 at www.gov.uk/government/publications/collective-worship-in-schools

Department for Education (2013) *National Curriculum for England: Framework for Key Stages 1 to 4*. London: DfE. Accessed on 24 May 2017 at www.gov.uk/government/publications/national-curriculum-in-england-framework-for-key-stages-1-to-4

Hansard (1988) *Education Reform Bill Debate, House of Lords. (Debate 3 May 1988, Vol 496, cc 413–421)*. London: Hansard. Accessed on 24 May 2017 at http://hansard.millbanksystems.com/lords/1988/may/03/education-reform-bill

Heelas, P. (2005) *The Spiritual Revolution: Why Religion Is Giving Way to Spirituality*. Hoboken, NJ: Wiley-Blackwell.

Heelas, P. and Woodhead, L. (2000) *Religion in Modern Times: An Interpretive Anthology*. Hoboken, NJ: Wiley-Blackwell.

Jackson, R. and O'Grady, K. (2007) 'Religions and Education in England: Social Plurality, Civil Religion and Religious Education Pedagogy.' In R. Jackson, S. Miedema, W. Weisse and J.-P. Willaime (eds) *Religion and Education in Europe: Developments, Contexts and Debates* (pp.181–202). Religious diversity and education in Europe (Bd.3). Münster: Waxmann.

Schools Council (1971) *Religious Education in Secondary Schools*. Working Paper 36. London: Methuen.

Smart, N. (1968) *Secular Education and the Logic of Religion*. London: Faber and Faber.

Chapter 2

A EUROPEAN PERSPECTIVE

*How Educational Reforms Influence
the Place and Image of RE*

PETER SCHREINER

*Two concerns guide me. The first is that we no longer can define
education by referring exclusively to a national context. Trends of a
Europeanisation of education and schooling and attendant global
developments influence concepts and concerns of education such as
quality, efficiency and outcome. The second is that we cannot speak
about religious education, either with small or with capital letters
(RE), without referring to these developments in general education
and in school education. Dominant trends and concepts of general
education and related policy provide a framework, and influence
the place and image of RE. From both perspectives, threats and
promises for RE arise.*

*First, I offer some insights in general trends in education policy;
and second, I introduce basic threats for RE. Finally, I will discuss
the findings and offer some promises for RE.*

Theoretical framework

As a theoretical framework, I refer to the theory of the Dutch
scholar Gert Biesta (2010, 2013). He differentiates between three
domains of educational purposes. The domain of qualification
has to do with the acquisition of knowledge, skills, values and
dispositions; socialisation 'has to do with the ways in which,

through education, we become part of existing traditions and ways of doing and being' (2013, p.4); and the domain of subjectivication deals with the subjectivity or 'subject-ness' of those we educate, their freedom and the related responsibility. This understanding sees education as an encounter between human beings and not as an interaction between machines. With the words of John Dewey we can also say: 'Education…is a process of living, and not a preparation for future living' (Dewey 1897, p.7).

Biesta (2010, p.50) describes a process in which the question of good education is being displaced by other questions, such as about measurement and evidence. In his view, these perspectives cannot sufficiently answer the question of what is educationally desirable. Biesta's view contradicts a dominant political understanding of education that puts more emphasis on qualification for the global labour market than on anything else. Global market-oriented qualification has become a key attainment target in education policy at national level and also for European institutions. I call it a dominant economic orientation of education and related policy.

Economic orientation of education policy

An economic orientation of education means that economic growth and competitiveness become the dominant drivers of education, while other goals become subordinated. Markers of this perspective are efficiency in public-sector institutions including schools, a pressure for accountability and a shift to market-based governance mechanisms (Afdal 2010; Ball 2008; Liessmann 2008; Miedema 2017; Münch 2009). This leaves states – which once controlled education in the name of nation-building, forming national citizens and nurturing social solidarity – in a minority position in a project driven by international economic demands and labour-market orientation.

PISA as a crucial example of the economic orientation

A crucial example and also a driving force of this trend is the Programme for International Student Assessment (PISA) of the Organisation for *Economic* Co-operation and Development (OECD) (my emphasis), which has risen to strategic prominence in international education policy debates (Meyer and Benavot 2013). PISA uses the general slogan 'Better Politics for a better life'. It was launched in 1997 as a triennial assessment, focusing on the core school subjects of science, reading and mathematics. One reason to establish PISA was the need for empirical data concerning excellence and equity as outcomes of education systems. The programme establishes a worldwide empirically based monitoring system and gives feedback for education systems. From the very beginning it has become important where in the tables a country is ranked. Average or low level is considered undesirable and shameful. In some countries PISA became a main force for educational reforms. It demonstrates a growing impact of the OECD on policy and practice in secondary schooling.

PISA has become the most comprehensive and rigorous international assessment of student knowledge and skills. The PISA 2015 Assessment and Analytical Framework presents the conceptual foundations of the sixth cycle of the triennial assessment. Similar to the previous cycles, the 2015 assessment covers science, reading and mathematics, with the major focus on scientific literacy this cycle. Financial literacy is evaluated as an optional assessment, as it was in 2012. A questionnaire about students' background is distributed to all participating students. Students may also choose to complete additional questionnaires: one about their future studies and career, a second about their familiarity with information and communication technologies. School principals complete a questionnaire about the learning environment in their schools, and parents of students who sit the PISA test can choose to complete a questionnaire about the home environment. Seventy-one countries and economies, including all 34 OECD countries, participated in the PISA 2015 assessment.

Meyer and Benavot (2013) present PISA/OECD as a crucial example for the emergence of global educational governance by large-scale international organisations. The role of PISA is important:

> in advancing a new mode of global education governance in which state sovereignty over educational matters is replaced by the influence of large-scale international organizations, and in which the very meaning of public education is being recast from a project aimed at forming national citizens and nurturing social solidarity to a project driven by economic demands and labor market orientations. (Meyer and Benavot 2013, p.10)

European education policy on life-long learning

What is documented for the OECD and their involvement in measuring outcomes of formal education processes can be confirmed by the policy of the European Union (EU). The EU has put a focus on research and development, education and life-long learning. This is part of the EU 2020 strategy on smart, sustainable and inclusive growth. The priorities of the strategy are:

- *Smart growth* – developing an economy based on knowledge and innovation

- *Sustainable growth* – promoting a more resource-efficient, greener and more competitive economy

- *Inclusive growth* – fostering a high-employment economy delivering social and territorial cohesion.

The terms sound nice but the strategy supports a trend to measure education with economic criteria. It is all about developing human capital or human resources.

The trigger and catalyst of a Europeanisation of education from the perspective of European institutions has been the decision of the European Council in 2000 to make Europe the most competitive and dynamic knowledge-based economy in the world, capable of sustainable economic growth with more and better jobs and greater social cohesion (European Council 2000).

Since then, activities in education and training have been established as integrated activities of European cooperation. Examples are the European Qualifications Framework, which joins the qualifications of different EU member states together for more transparency, comparison and mobility, and the Strategic Framework for Education and Training (ET 2020) as a guiding policy document for education and training in the EU member states. ET 2020 is a forum for exchanges of best practice, mutual learning, gathering and dissemination of information, and evidence of what works, as well as advice and support for policy reforms. It is based on a set of four common EU objectives to address challenges in education and training systems by 2020:

- Making life-long learning and mobility a reality

- Improving the quality and efficiency of education and training

- Promoting equity, social cohesion and active citizenship

- Enhancing creativity and innovation, including entre-preneurship, at all levels of education and training.

The third crucial tool of European education policy is Erasmus+, the EU programme for education, training, youth and sports with a budget of €14.7 billion for 2014 to 2020. It enables exchange of different students and experts in the fields of schools, universities, training, sports and youth, and encourages European exchange and cooperation towards a European identity.

As already stated, European and international organisations have a great commitment in education. European policies influence national policies and lead to the transformation of state systems. The term 'Europeanisation' is used to describe the interplay of EU integration and change in member countries (Dale 2009; Radaelli 2003; Schreiner 2012). The vertical dimension of Europeanisation refers to the policy of European institutions; the horizontal dimension refers to exchange and comparison between different national or local contexts (Beck and Grande 2004).

Although a comprehensive and multiplex understanding of what education means can be recognised in some of these developments, there are stronger trends towards an economics-based Europeanisation of education. I discuss two documents that can underline this perspective. The first comes from the European Commission. They launched a Communication to the European Parliament and other European bodies to encourage a fundamental shift in education policy. The document is called *Rethinking Education: Investing in Skills for Better Socio-Economic Outcomes* (2012). To be fair to the document it should be noted that also in this text a 'broad mission' of education is mentioned encompassing objectives 'such as active citizenship, personal development and well-being' (p.2), but the main focus of the paper is on the economic key concerns of productivity and growth. This can be underlined by the following extract:

> European education and training systems continue to fall short in providing the right skills for employability, and are not working adequately with business or employers to bring the learning experience closer to the reality of the working environment. These skills mismatches are a growing concern for European industry's competitiveness. (European Commission 2012, p.2)

This is a harsh critique of the education and training systems of Europe. Employability and competitiveness are chief concerns throughout the whole statement and education is functionalised for these purposes.

The point that education should prepare young people for the job market is not wrong. It is important, but it becomes bizarre when human beings are valued as human capital or human resources according to economic scales, and not treated as humans as such. From a Christian perspective, shared also by other religions, everyone is created in the image of God and should not be measured according to his or her competence or achievement in a job.

The second document introduces the well-known Erasmus+ programme (mentioned above), which has become a crucial instrument for promoting a European identity and for promoting a feeling that we all are European. Nevertheless the policy of Erasmus+ is based on elements of an economic orientation.

The online Erasmus+ Programme Guide (European Commission 2016) includes the following statement:

> Europe needs more cohesive and inclusive societies, which allow citizens to play an active role in democratic life. Education and youth work are key to promote common European values, foster social integration, enhance intercultural understanding and a sense of belonging to a community, and to prevent violent radicalisation. Erasmus+ is an effective instrument to promote the inclusion of people with disadvantaged backgrounds, including newly arrived migrants. ...
>
> Well-performing education and training systems and youth policies provide people with the *skills required by the labour market and the economy*, while allowing them to play an active role in society and achieve personal fulfilment. Reforms in education, training and youth can strengthen progress towards these goals, on the basis of a shared vision between policy makers and stakeholders, sound evidence and cooperation across different fields and levels...
>
> This investment in *knowledge, skills and competences* will benefit individuals, institutions, organisations and society as a whole by *contributing to growth* and ensuring equity, prosperity and social inclusion in Europe and beyond. (European Commission 2016, my emphasis)

A critical view on these developments is needed also when we reflect on the situation of Religious Education.

Competition of education systems

The economic orientation includes issues of effectiveness and quality of teaching. The EU has introduced the Open Method of Cooperation (OMC) between member states in the field of education that nurtures a competition among them. OMC provides a trend to compare the success of education systems. It consists of the following elements:

- Fixing guidelines for the Union combined with specific timetables

- Establishing indicators and benchmarks such as the percentage of early school leavers

- Translating European guidelines into national and regional policies

- Periodic monitoring, evaluation and peer review as mutual learning processes.

OMC is used as a tool that does not contradict the structural and content-based responsibility of the member states in the area of education, but systematically circumvents it by agreements on indicators of success, quality and efficiency of the education and training systems.

From input to outcome orientation

This goes along with a general change of the main paradigm in education. Education processes are no longer oriented to the transmission of content but based on measurable acquisition of knowledge, skills and attitudes. The focus shifted from the issue of how curricula and syllabuses are designed to the question of what the outcome is of schooling and educational activities.

The new buzzword is 'competence'. The term is used differently. In general it refers to knowledge, skills and attitudes for developing understanding. A broad understanding is positive because more than knowledge is required; yet the ambivalence appears when it is asked: What measurable competences do we have after a period of teaching and learning?

Economic crisis and education policy

We face the problem of an increasing commodification and economisation of education, fuelled by both the growing importance of knowledge in industry, and the diminishing public funds for the educational sector. This has led to a situation where higher education institutions increasingly run as corporate entities. The knowledge-based economy has provided an easy means of establishing education, and its resulting degrees and qualifications, as a resource that can be commoditised.

Nico Hirtt (2011) shows the complexity of related processes and dynamics. He connects the economic crisis and the need for innovation with developments of the global labour market, with the related activities of the state and with education policy. His main ideas are that material economic circumstances push the education systems toward marketisation. In his view, education policy is influenced by the state and the (global) labour market. I introduce his approach to demonstrate the complexity of the issue of an economisation of education.

Hirtt states that the material economic circumstances push the education systems in advanced capitalist countries toward marketisation. The concept of marketisation should be understood in a broad sense. It means not only increasing privatisation, transforming education into new markets; it also means a narrow adaptation of education to the specific demands of labour markets; and it means using education systems as an instrument to stimulate markets, especially the ICT-markets.

Basic threats for RE

My first section provided the wider context in which Religious Education is embedded. I shall now have a closer look at the situation of RE to identify challenges and threats. I do not mean to imply a cause-and-effect relationship between an economic orientation of education and the image and value of RE. It may be that both areas are related in a complex way, and describing threats for RE could make aspects of this relation a bit more obvious and plausible.

A first line of argumentation refers to aims of RE in RE curricula and syllabuses across Europe. Although approaches are different owing to the different layers that shape the context for RE (Schreiner 2014), the following list of aims can be presented as a core concern: religious literacy, religious orientation, knowledge, competence, identity development, exploration of personal and organised worldviews, and social instrumental aims of RE (e.g. fighting extremism and hate speech, social cohesion, citizenship) (Grimmitt 2010).

Religious Education stands for speaking about awe and wonder, for introducing different perceptions of life, for learning through religions that are more than cultural facts, especially in the view of believers.

In school the competition between hard-core subjects and soft subjects continues. Competences, economic needs, human capital, employability, flexibility, mobility; these are well-established priorities in the educational discourse and often dominate the intentions of RE.

Against the background of the trends toward an economisation of education, introduced in the first part of this chapter, I will briefly discuss four threats for RE, not as an exclusive or complete list but as an invitation to think about how RE is affected by these trends:

- Dominance of a limited concept of education

- Marginalisation of RE in the school curriculum

- Changes in the inner structure and in the image of RE

- Perception of students.

Limited concept of education

A limited concept of education dominates, oriented more or less on economic needs, exemplified by terms such as employability, flexibility and mobility, human capital or human resources, and less on aspects of personal development and identity formation. These often influence government policy toward RE by neglecting or not paying enough attention to the subject.

The example of England is obvious and well documented. In the recent Review of Religious Education in England, large-scale changes in education policy are mentioned:

> These include the introduction of the English Baccalaureate, towards whose achievement GCSE Religious Studies cannot be counted, significant reforms of GCSE and A Level qualifications, the extension of the academies programme and introduction of free schools, all of which have implications for the way in which RE and its curriculum are decided and supported. Local authority cuts have also led to the reduction of local support for RE, and the number of new trainee teachers has been slashed. The total number of GCSE Religious Studies entries has started to decline after many years of growth. (Religious Education Council 2013, p.7)

This appalling list documents that the priority is not on RE but on other concerns. Conditions for RE are becoming worse. This happens also in other countries that follow this limited concept of education.

Marginalisation of RE in the school curriculum

In many countries, trends toward a marginalisation of RE are obvious. Other subjects are valued as more important than RE.

A current example is Luxembourg where the existing confessional RE, in combination with an alternative subject of Ethics/Morals, was replaced in 2016. Instead, a subject called 'Life and Society' was introduced in all secondary schools. The explanation for the installation of the new obligatory subject is:

> Why a new subject? The cultural background of children and young people is becoming more and more diverse. This includes also the religious convictions of the families. The public school must provide a space of dialogue, in which living together can be developed and respect in dealing with diversity can be transmitted. 'Life and society' therefore brings all students together in a course. (Le Gouvernement du Grand-Duché de Luxembourg 2016)

Aims of the new subject are promotion of tolerance (based on knowledge), critical-reflective discussion and understanding of the big questions of life and society. Obviously the former approach of RE was no longer appreciated and was seen as inadequate to reach these aims. For me, this description of aims should also be an expectation for all existing forms of Religious Education.

Changes in the inner structure and image of RE

A limited concept of education and processes of marginalisation of RE led also to changes in the inner structure and image of RE. In many countries, the number of RE lessons was reduced (in Sweden secondary level to one hour per fortnight), and often RE is taught on the margin of the school day. In England, the Ofsted report (2013) discusses as areas of concern low standards, weak teaching, problems in developing a curriculum for RE and confusion about the purpose of RE. A lack of subject knowledge by teachers and a reduction of teaching facilities are symptoms of the subject being given less value than other subjects.

Perception of students

It is no wonder that also the perception of students is influenced by the deplorable situation of RE. Many of them do not see RE as a serious subject but a break between, say, Maths and French. This might be a consequence of the wider situation for RE. When the status of a subject differs from other subjects, can you expect from students that they take it seriously?

Conclusion

Educational reforms and a focus on economic criteria for school education create threats and challenges for Religious Education. This happens in the European contexts, as the examples have shown. Initiatives are needed to show the value and importance of RE and to argue for its equal integration in the school curricula. In England it is the need for parity with the subjects of the National Curriculum. A number of reports from different agencies and organisations about the current situation of RE include critical remarks (e.g. All Party Parliamentary Group on RE 2013; Clarke and Woodhead 2015; Commission on Religion and Belief in British Public Life 2015).

The review of RE in England, especially its six recommendations for structuring and sustaining RE in the 21st century, are finally mentioned as an example on how improvement may be possible. These recommendations (RE Council 2013, p.32) are to:

- Support improvement by developing more effective and coherent mechanisms to monitor and evaluate the effectiveness of RE.

- Pursue with policy makers the challenges around the existing 'settlement' for RE.

- Promote coherence and progression between pro-grammes of study for 4–14-year-olds and public examinations for 14–19-year-olds.

- Ensure that there are more robust arrangements for training and supporting teachers of RE.

- Develop new structures and networks within and across the RE community so that its expertise is coordinated and utilised more effectively in the interests of improving the subject.

- Develop new assessment arrangements for RE.

A new, more energetic position for RE to some extent depends on a new, more human-centred vision for education.

References

Afdal, G. (2010) *Researching Religious Education as Social Practice*. Series on Religious Diversity and Education in Europe, 20. Münster: Waxmann.

All Party Parliamentary Group on RE (2013) *RE: The Truth Unmasked*. Accessed on 25 May 2017 at http://religiouseducationcouncil.org.uk/media/file/APPG_RE_-_The_Truth_Unmasked.pdf

Ball, S.J. (2008) *The Education Debate*. Bristol: Policy Press.

Beck, U. and Grande, E. (2004) *Das Kosmopolitische Europa* [The Cosmopolitical Europe]. Frankfurt am Main: Suhrkamp.

Biesta, G. (2010) *Good Education in an Age of Measurement: Ethics, Politics, Democracy*. New York, NY and Abingdon: Routledge.

Biesta, G. (2013) *The Beautiful Risk of Education*. Boulder, CO: Paradigm Publishers.

Clarke, C. and Woodhead, L. (2015) *A New Settlement: Religion and Belief in Schools*. Lancaster University: Westminster Faith Debates. Accessed on 25 May 2017 at http://faithdebates.org.uk/wp-content/uploads/2015/06/A-New-Settlement-for-Religion-and-Belief-in-schools.pdf

Commission on Religion and Belief in British Public Life (2015) *Living with Difference: Community, Diversity and the Common Good*. Accessed on 25 May 2017 at www.woolf.cam.ac.uk/uploads/Living with Difference.pdf

Dale, R. (2009) *Globalisation and Europeanisation in Education*. Oxford: Symposium Books.

Dewey, J. (1897) *My Pedagogic Creed*. Accessed on 25 May 2017 at https://en.wikisource.org/wiki/My_Pedagogic_Creed#ARTICLE_TWO._WHAT_THE_SCHOOL_IS

European Commission (2012) *Rethinking Education: Investing in Skills for Better Socio-economic Outcomes*. Accessed on 25 May 2017 at http://eur-lex.europa.eu/legal-content/EN/TXT/PDF/?uri=CELEX:52012DC0669&from=EN

European Commission (2016) *Erasmus+ Programme Guide*. Accessed on 25 June 2017 at http://ec.europa.eu/programmes/erasmus-plus/programme-guide/part-a_en

European Council (2000) *Lisbon European Council, 23 and 24 March 2000, Presidency Conclusions.* Accessed on 25 June 2017 at http://www.europarl. europa.eu/summits/lis1_en.htm

Grimmitt, M. (2010) 'Contributing to Social and Community Cohesion: Just Another Stage in the Metamorphosis of Religious Education? – An Extended End Piece.' In M. Grimmitt (ed.) *Religious Education and Social and Community Cohesion: An Exploration of Challenges and Opportunities* (pp.260–317). Great Wakering: McCrimmons.

Hirtt, N. (2011) 'Education in the "Knowledge Economy": Consequences for Democracy.' In L. Ludwig, H. Luckas, F. Hamburger and S. Aufenanger (eds) *Bildung in der Demokratie II. Tendenzen-Diskurse-Praktiken* (pp.167–176). Opladen and Farmington Hills, MI: Barbara Budrich.

Le Gouvernement du Grand-Duché de Luxembourg, Ministère de l'Education nationale, de l'Enfance et de la Jeunesse (2016) *Vie et Societé Leben und Gesellschaft Vida e Sociedade, Information for Parents.* Accessed on 25 May 2017 at www.men.public.lu/catalogue-publications/secondaire/ informations-generales-offre-scolaire/VieSo-Elterninformationen/ Elterninformationen.pdf

Liessmann, P. (2008) *Theorie der Unbildung* (A Theory of De-education). München: Piper.

Meyer, H.-D. and Benavot, A. (2013) *PISA, Power and Policy: The Emergence of Global Educational Governance.* Oxford: Symposium Books.

Miedema, S. (2017) 'Bildung in Zeiten des Wandels: Konturen und Herausforderungen.' [Education in times of change: Contours and challenges). *Zeitschrift für Pädagogik und Theologie 69*, 1, 82–91.

Münch, R. (2009) *Globale Eliten, Lokale Autoritäten: Bildung und Wissenschaft unter dem Regime von PISA, McKinsey & Co.* [Global Elites, Local Authorities: Education and Science under the Regime of PISA, McKinsey & Co.]. Frankfurt am Main: Suhrkamp.

Ofsted (2013) *Religious Education: Realising the Potential.* Accessed on 25 May 2017 at www.gov.uk/government/publications/religious-education-realising-the-potential

Radaelli, C.M. (2003) 'The Europeanization of Public Politics.' In. K. Featherstone and C.M. Radaelli (eds) *The Politics of Europeanization* (pp.27–56). Oxford: Oxford University Press.

Religious Education Council (2013) *A Review of Religious Education in England.* London: RE Council.

Schreiner, P. (2012) *Religion im Kontext einer Europäisierung von Bildung* [Religion in the Context of a Europeanisation of Education]. Münster: Waxmann.

Schreiner, P. (2014) 'Religious Education in Europe.' In M. Rothgangel, T. Schlag and F. Schweitzer (eds) *Basics of Religious Education* (pp.161–177). Göttingen and Bristol, CN: V & R Unipress.

Chapter 3

RELIGIOUS EDUCATION AND THE 'KNOWLEDGE PROBLEM'

RICHARD KUEH

The reason why Religious Education is in crisis is that it continues to be plagued by a significant and unresolved knowledge problem. Against a backdrop of the subject's own legacy, wherein justification for a Religious Education curriculum has navigated and appealed to a variety of different (broadly speaking) non-knowledge-based rationales (from spiritual encounter, to social capital, to the development of the whole human in a democratic context), RE has been unsuccessful in finding strong, coherent consensus about the status, function and utility of knowledge within it. If there is any hope of finding a workable model for RE, then practitioners and theoreticians must recognise the urgent need to gain momentum behind an agreed understanding of the knowledge that it confers.

This piece explores various rationales for curriculum expression that have been linked to RE. Whilst acknowledging their value, I suggest that the multiplicity of rationales detracts attention from the important debate about knowledge within RE. Moreover, from within the field of RE practitioners, the case is made that a historical intertwining of rationale and pedagogy has unhelpfully generated further proliferation of complexity to the knowledge problem.

The chapter then explores concepts of 'deep' and 'powerful' knowledge, in contradistinction to reductive essentialist notions of knowledge. The chapter culminates in an argument demonstrating that a renewed focus on the status of knowledge within RE will lead to a more pedagogically and politically potent case for the place of RE in the curriculum, and that, in doing so, the subject will find itself satisfying increasing demands for intellectual rigour.

Chained to the past: The knowledge problem as RE's own legacy

We need to talk about knowledge. Religious Education is clearly in the political and educational spotlight, facing an unprecedented degree of political scrutiny. A significant part of the scrutiny it has faced originates in questions about its academic rigour and intellectual pedigree: this became manifestly clear during the debates about its non-inclusion within the English Baccalaureate in 2012. In turn, this directly relates to the question of the knowledge at the heart of the subject. No wonder there is still widespread public uncertainty about the nature and purpose of RE (Religious Education Council 2013). So we, as advocates and practitioners of RE, need to talk about knowledge.

Marx once wrote that the 'traditions of dead generations weigh like a nightmare on the minds of the living' (1852/1926, p.23). Whilst it is important to acknowledge with gratitude the efforts of those within the RE community who have risen to the challenge in their respective eras (and from their particular vantage points) of responding to the needs of learners' religious understanding, the complexity of that legacy, in a number of important respects, leaves a 'nightmarish' state for RE today. Certainly, that historical complexity has led to the circumstances wherein the general public is uncertain of RE's function and, furthermore, where there is a lack of understanding of, and support for, RE among senior school leaders and policy-makers (Religious Education Council 2013).

Of course, the complexity of the rationale for RE as a disciplinary subject in England pre-dates the 1944 Education Act: it is intertwined with collective worship in school, the religious origins of education and the social history of the Church. Yet, in many ways, the ongoing and widespread uncertainty about the nature and purpose of RE has stemmed from the fact that significant and influential pedagogies offered for RE from the 1960s onwards have been influenced by these (historically speaking) confessional origins of the subject. Many pedagogies were characterised by 'Liberal Christian, Theological, Experimental, Implicit Models' (Grimmitt 2000, p.26). The two main attainment targets, 'learning about' and 'learning from', contain within them generic, overly optimistic, liberal assumptions about religion, derived from the confessional past, which are becoming increasingly defective and unreliable. These assumptions are problematic precisely because they assume that one can and should learn from every form of religious expression. This notion is fundamentally rooted in positivistic assumptions about religion. Learning from becomes particularly problematic in a post-apartheid, post-9/11, post-ISIS/Daesh, post-Brexit, post-Trump, global landscape where the various (and darker) facets of religion and belief need to be accounted for within a framework of understanding, just as much as the brighter ones.

However, alternative voices within RE's historical tradition, which established themselves as undogmatic and in contradistinction to the experiential model of religion within RE, were not without problems. Teaching religions as phenomena (often associated with the work of Ninian Smart), with the widespread popular assumption that there could be an absolute existential distance between the interpreter and the subject matter (an assumption disavowed by Smart and many phenomenological colleagues), fails to account for the complexity of the way in which religion, history and culture are intertwined. In severing so completely the links between the learner and religious subject matter, this approach does not really incorporate the complex interplay of learner, history, culture and subject matter; it fails to explain the significance or importance, for the learner, of studying that subject matter.

So against this historical backdrop, with traditions that focus on the experiential encounter with religion or unhelpfully assume positive possibilities in learning from religious expressions, or indeed that divorce learners so completely from the subject matter such that it raises the whole question of subject-rationale, one can understand why there is such a degree of confusion about the nature and purpose of the knowledge that might be obtained from RE. In a historical sense, the circumstances that generated confessional approaches to RE pedagogy – and indeed the circumstances that led to a reaction against them – are accidental. However, to anchor the purpose of RE in a set of historical circumstances that no longer pertain in the UK is not helpful. Instead, we need to talk about a contemporary and clear rationale for RE that demonstrates the disciplinary knowledge-base within it.

Rationales for curriculum expression

To solve the knowledge problem, the solution to which, I accept, is by no means self-evident, there needs to be a prominent, strong and contemporary case articulated for the curricular rationale for Religious Education. This involves decoupling the RE debate from its historical roots in forms of schooling that we have left behind, and focusing on the present.

A helpful departure point (expounded in much greater detail in Kueh 2014, p.9) is to consider three main motifs of curricular expression. These are 'ways' of expressing the curriculum that give substance and meaning to the case made for why any particular subject might be taught:

- An instrumental curriculum as a means to some overall end

- An enrichment curriculum that relates to the general flourishing of humans

- A knowledge-based curriculum that focuses upon the intrinsic value of that knowledge.

Allies and advocates of RE instinctively appeal to the first and second forms of curricular expression over and above the third. The result of this is that the intrinsic knowledge-basis for RE remains either unclear or unexpressed. In what follows, I will explore some of the work that has been done in respect of imagining RE within an 'instrumental curriculum' and in an 'enrichment curriculum', before proceeding to offer some reflections on the principles of a 'knowledge-based curriculum' for RE.

An instrumental curriculum as a means to some overall end

The 'instrumental' value of a curriculum subject focuses its rationale, in a utilitarian fashion, on some kind of beneficial outcome. It is a curriculum framed as a means to further socio-economic interests which has been the dominant rationale for education in recent years. Prompted by a neo-liberal argument that governmental economic activity should be vastly diminished in favour of leaving the free market to shape the economy (a stance taken increasingly by educational policy in Thatcher, Major and Blair governments), the case was made that schools needed to respond to the demands of the economy. Critics pointed out that, in this model, the very values of educational professionals were implicitly undermined in playing the economic market game, forging dichotomies like serving community/attracting clients, collectivism/competition and intrinsic value/costs and outcomes (Ball 2006). The case for economic instrumentalism was politically persuasive, and the political dedication to gearing schools vocationally towards producing economically useful leavers continued to shape the focus and content of the school curriculum (Beck 2008).

How might one justify Religious Education *instrumentally*, as a means of furthering the economy? The All Party Parliamentary Group on RE (APPG 2013, 2014) have highlighted the important role of RE within the curriculum. Their recent work to some extent exemplifies a 'utility' concept of curriculum justification. For them, the study of RE within schools can reduce religious misunderstandings and social conflicts within communities. According to the APPG, RE is a 'strong contributor to good community relations' (APPG 2014, p.1). In this way, RE helps young people to leave school with an accurate grasp of the relevance of religion and enables students to make informed choices.

Put another way, this position is, using the terminology of Robert D. Putnam, a case for 'social capital'. Putnam explains the concept as distinct from 'physical' capital (material objects) or 'human' capital (human beings and their various characteristics and properties), as a sort of valuable commodity generated from the interactions between individuals in certain conditions: 'social capital refers to connections among individuals – social networks and the norms of reciprocity and trustworthiness that arise from them' (Putnam 2000, p.19). Putnam's ideas conjure the image of an intricate woven tapestry. The tapestry image is important as it is the relational aspect of social capital that distinguishes it from mere civic virtue:

> The difference is that 'social capital' calls attention to the fact that civic virtue is most powerful when embedded in a sense network of reciprocal social relations. A society of many virtuous but isolated individuals is not necessarily rich in social capital. (Putnam 2000, p.19)

Social capital is a form of interwoven interaction between individuals within communities, which enables their building and strengthening from within, based on a dynamic of reciprocity and a certain type of commitment between people. The work of the APPG can be understood within this context to suggest that Religious Education performs an extremely valuable function of stabilising, bridging, bonding and linking within society. For the APPG, RE performs its function when it is able to 'promote open-mindedness and an informed perspective on religions and worldviews' (APPG 2014, p.3). This, in turn, links to notions of economic advantage, since a stable society, secure and protected from the volatility of friction between sub-groups within it, offers an established and confident basis for prosperous economic development.

An enrichment curriculum which relates to the general flourishing of humans

In recent years, John White has been a staunch advocate of this second way of framing the curriculum, considering that it be shaped around an individual's wellbeing and personal flourishing (White 2007). He contends that mere economic instrumentalism 'has a poor understanding of fulfilment' (p.32). For him, personal fulfilment is understood as social and civic involvement, a contribution to the economy and the fostering of practical wisdom, based upon the recognition that success often involves 'good practical judgement' (p.29). All this takes place within a context of 'democratic citizenship' (White 2007, p.25).

The American philosopher Martha Nussbaum's recent work on the humanities bears a resemblance to this sort of justification in respect of Religious Education. For her, democratic citizenship and personal fulfilment are cognate motifs that complement her case that there is great meaning and importance in the study of religion and belief. Nussbaum (2010) makes a powerful case that there is a long-term cost to democracy when governments and nations cut back on the humanities. She contends that the economy's surreptitious dominance in politics and culture has focused the vision of education far too narrowly, which has culminated in a current crisis:

> The humanities and arts are being cut away, in both primary/ secondary and college/university education, in virtually every nation of the world. Seen by policy-makers as useless frills, at a time when nations must cut away all useless things in order to stay competitive in the global market, they are rapidly losing

their place in curricula, and also in the minds and hearts of parents and children. Indeed, what we might call the humanistic aspect of science and social science – the imaginative, creative aspect, and the aspect of rigorous critical thought – are also losing ground as nations prefer to pursue short-term profit by the cultivation of the useful and highly applied skills suited to profit-making. The crisis is facing us, but we have not yet faced it. (Nussbaum 2010, p.2)

Nussbaum's position is anchored in the notion that curricula need to develop the human in holistic terms, not narrowly predetermine their focus towards industrial conceptions of utility and profit. She wishes curricula to cultivate 'the faculties of thought and imagination', which, she believes, 'make our relationships rich human relationships', instead of 'relationships of mere use and manipulation' (Nussbaum 2010, p.6). The possible long-term effects of a dominant economic focus on human self-reflection are so often ignored or glossed over. By contrast, it is Nussbaum's assertion that successful, fruitful and nourishing democracy requires a certain type of self-examination and critical ability afforded by the type of study enshrined in humanities subjects like RE. For example, RE develops cultural-historical skills in students, which helps them avoid the narrow stereotyping of religions and which is of utmost importance given the very complex interconnection of religion and global current issues.

The work of these RE allies provides extremely useful examples of contemporary rationales for Religious Education. They stress different emphases: the former demonstrates that RE does indeed yield social and economic benefits but not of a reductive sort; the latter argues that without the humanities democracy as a whole suffers. However, both engage critically and seriously with concepts of curriculum justification, such as value, enrichment, democracy, self-examination, cost–benefit and economic advantage. Yet it is still not necessarily clear what place extensive subject-specific disciplinary knowledge has within RE. In this sense, the issue of knowledge in relation to Religious Education is still an outstanding one. Put another way: it is not self-evidently clear what precise pieces or types of knowledge benefit bridging and bonding within society. Nor is it clear, perhaps due to the gulf between the micro-scale planning of day-to-day lessons and the macro-scale goal of mass-societal democratic self-reflection, what the knowledge-base for this particular enterprise should be.

'Powerful knowledge' and the curriculum

If we are able to get the knowledge-base for RE clear, if we can explain the intrinsic value of RE knowledge, and if (in other words) we can 'solve the knowledge problem', then the complementary benefits for RE (rich social capital within our communities, civic virtue and democratic self-awareness) will flow organically from that.

Framing the curriculum in terms of pure knowledge and viewing its value as important 'in and of itself' has been championed politically in recent years. Prominent voices appeal to an educational essentialist position, most notably through the work of educationalist and literary critic E.D. Hirsch, Jr, whose work (Hirsch 1987) argued that learners require essential pieces of knowledge that literate communicators assume their addressees to possess. Editions of the work, for example, included lists of five thousand essential dates, phrases, ideas and snap biographies for the benefit of its readers. Hirsch's work went on to influence government policy on education in England. Michael Gove, formerly a Secretary of State for Education, pronounced himself 'an unashamed traditionalist when it comes to the curriculum...with children sitting in rows, learning the kings and queens of England' (quoted in Haydn 2010, p.33). Nick Gibb, a long-serving Minister of State in Education, discussed the ways in which Hirsch influenced both himself and Gove on education policy within the 2010 Coalition government (Gibb 2015). That same government chose not to include RE as a subject on the Baccalaureate. The move was controversial and promoted much discussion, including about whether RE was perceived to have the same academic status as, for example, History and Geography (see Long and Bolton 2017).

However, this is by no means the only way of developing a knowledge-based curriculum. Michael Young offers an alternative vision for justifying aspects of the curriculum on the grounds of knowledge. Young speaks of 'powerful knowledge' (Young 2009, 2010, 2011), a concept that rejects two opposite ends of a spectrum: it rejects the assumptions of educational essentialists who seem to assume the a-social given-ness of knowledge (they accept that the body of knowledge to be studied is to some degree self-evident, which Young believes is a huge assumption); but powerful knowledge also rejects the opposite idea of radical social constructivists that knowledge is in essence a mere social construct. If it is, according to Young, then even determinate factors in knowledge-content become 'arbitrary', since they are mere 'responses to political pressures' (Young 2011, p.269).

Young describes his position as that of a 'social realist', where he rejects an epistemology that is 'under-socialised' (one that essentially denies or ignores the embeddedness of knowledge within society); equally he rejects an epistemology that is 'over-socialised' (one that essentially reduces knowledge to the identities of communities). For him, powerful knowledge is not reducible to communities, contexts and its social origins, but certainly does emerge from within them (Young and Muller 2010, p.14).

Young believes that there is a core body of knowledge that students should know, and that this is supremely central to the identity and purposes of schools (shared with Hirsch); but he also believes that this knowledge is simultaneously linked to sociological factors (shared with social constructivists). He claims that 'the model I am arguing for also treats knowledge as external to learners, it recognises that this externality is not given, but has a social and historical basis' (Young 2010, p.22).

It is for this reason that Young's view of powerful knowledge is so curriculo-centric, but also holds firmly on to the belief that the knowledge must genuinely be demonstrated on strong socio-historical grounds to be relevant to all individuals.

The type of knowledge that Young prescribes as the basis for the school curriculum is subject-specific, but also dependent upon wider trends in historical, cultural and scientific progress, as opposed to short-term economic trends (Young 2009). Subjects as discrete areas of expertise cannot be diluted, because each subject area contains dual aspects of importance: subjects have specific contextual applications (for mathematics it might be numerical proficiency in business; for English it might be critical examination of daily newspapers) but also general theoretical components that have the potential to impact human life in other ways (for example mathematics in macro-economics or astrophysics; English in the understanding of rhetoric and human linguistic expression). These general theoretical components are the basis on which one can delineate subjects. Subjects are themselves 'sets of regulated theoretical concepts' that confer 'the knowledge we need to live in society' (Young 2014, p.99), as well as being 'the forms of social organization that bring subject specialists together and give them their identities' (p.100).

Michael Young's concept of 'powerful knowledge' and his framework for considering the 'boundaries' of knowledge is both helpful and challenging for Religious Education. It is helpful as it gives academic legitimacy to a subject discipline that navigates beliefs, practices, truth claims, self-understandings, cultures, traditions and narratives. The specialist, disciplinary and conceptual knowledge that materialises from this multifaceted matrix is clearly significant knowledge because it is part of the social fabric of knowledge that has derived from global human history, but is also not necessarily reducible to the communities from which this knowledge emerges. In this sense, it promises assistance to help deal with RE's knowledge problem. The challenge comes in articulating that knowledge-based rationale and, moreover, empowering the RE community and schools with widespread understanding of the powerful knowledge that undergirds Religious Education's intrinsic worth on the curriculum.

'Powerful knowledge' and Religious Education

How might we fuse this important discussion with Religious Education? I will now attempt to draw out some of those features of powerful knowledge which are implicitly valuable to RE, and endeavour to make an explicit and unequivocal case for why they might help to solve RE's knowledge problem. In what follows, I wish to articulate five principles, which I hope go some way to providing a manifesto and rationale for developing a powerful knowledge-base for RE.

First, powerful knowledge in RE *brings substantive knowledge into the realm of disciplinary knowledge through concepts.* In other words, content is important, but concepts are paramount. 'Powerful knowledge' could be understood as the process whereby *substantive knowledge* (knowledge that is meaningfully 'basic' in that it is required in order to build on within the discipline of RE) is enhanced and developed into *disciplinary knowledge* (knowledge that constitutes a degree of specialism in the field of philosophical and theological discourse). This whole process is unlocked, importantly, through *substantive concepts.* Supporters of RE acknowledge and recognise this: the 2014 APPG report maintains that, whilst wide content about religious beliefs and practices (i.e. substantive knowledge) is valuable to a degree, it is 'not just content' that will lead to 'an informed perspective on religions and worldviews' (APPG 2014, p.3). Young too acknowledges that content 'is important', although 'not as facts to be memorized', but 'because without it students cannot acquire concepts and, therefore, will not develop their understanding' (Young 2014, p.97). The importance of concepts as the way to unlock the academic grounding of RE is gaining greater recognition. Mary Earl's recent work for the Woolf Institute in generating a concept-based toolkit for RE practitioners aims at focusing on concepts (she calls them 'lenses') thereby 'reframing Religious Education (RE) so that we align it as closely as possible to other subjects on the school curriculum' (Earl 2015, p.4).

Second, powerful knowledge in RE is rooted in the way the world is. Young's work shows that *knowledge that has the capacity to change is not something that is trans-temporal or a-social*: it is not something that we can universally lift out of history or remove from culture. Instead, it is embedded within the history and state of the world; it is rooted in the way things are. So if powerful knowledge is socially and historically embedded, then the *boundary of the knowledge that should be taught within RE at school needs to be defined by the global and historical patterns of religion and belief.* As the APPG puts it, '[p]atterns of belief, practice and adherence are changing locally, nationally and globally in ways that need to be reflected in the RE curriculum' (APPG 2014, p.3). In accepting this, we safeguard against two polarised possibilities: on the one hand, against the possibility that RE is reduced to an under-socialised knowledge (e.g. 'all Sikhs sit on the floors of Gurdwaras and eat vegetarian food'), which is unfaithful to their identities as living faiths; on the other hand, against the possibility of dismissing religion altogether on over-socialised grounds (e.g. by overlooking *global* and *historical* patterns of the growth of religious followers and merely observing patterns of secularisation *in the West* and *in the first decade or so of the 21st century*). Powerful knowledge lifts one's eyes from the here and now to the global and historical. Having safeguarded against both of these, the onus of responsibility about the selection of knowledge lies with practitioners to ensure that what is taught is an honest reflection of the global and historical reach of religion, faith and belief.

Third, powerful knowledge in RE confronts the questions of truth, evidence and proof and how these, in turn, come to bear on meaning. This is important as a precursor to any link between respect and Religious Education. Fostering respect for others as humans is a civic virtue (or social capital) and should not be conflated with a relativistic assumption that all truth claims enjoy the same status *vis-à-vis* truth. (This might, in Young's terms, be perceived as falling into an over-socialised epistemology.) So powerful knowledge in RE accepts the possibility that truth claims can be comparatively, critically and competitively juxtaposed in a critical realism framework (Young and Muller 2010). This framework is rooted in the work and philosophy of Roy Bhaskar (2010) and is developed by Andrew Wright (2015).

Fourth, powerful knowledge in RE requires critical engagement with the concepts of identity and culture as they relate to human meaning. These concepts are not arbitrary ones, but are anchored in the fact that specialist disciplinary understanding of beliefs and practices cannot be disentangled from the (internal) question of being, identity and the understanding of the self and the (external) question of how space and place shape the way in which humans understand the world meaningfully. Indeed, the very nature of powerful knowledge, with its emphasis on the situatedness of knowledge, recognises that religious and philosophical discourse throughout history has created some shared subject matter, so that shared subject matter will always stand in relation to beliefs and practices. This includes an understanding of the self, its meaning and its worth; the notion of finitude, temporality and existence; the idea of 'goodness' and leading of the 'good' life; the narratives within which beliefs inhabit and how they impact their adherents; and the way in which beliefs relate to environment and land and, in turn, the ways in which the narratives of belief affect the current and historical geo-political landscape.

Finally, powerful knowledge in RE recognises that learners are citizens of an inherently diverse world. It recognises the significance of different forms of belief-expression for billions of people and has the humility to accept that this belief-expression will always be pluriform, diverse, different, subtle and influential on the lives of people and, furthermore, that it cannot easily be categorised and packaged. In this way, the truly diverse composition of the world can be understood and, with it, the complexities that emerge at the juxtapositional fault-lines of belief-expression wherever and whenever they meet. (This in itself is advantageous socio-economically.) In order to achieve this, the various facets and shades of religion and belief need to be truly recognised as well as critiqued. Just as we should be dissatisfied with over-simplistic positivistic descriptions of beliefs, we should also be dissatisfied with any attempt to dismiss or to ignore the darker sides of human beliefs.

Conclusion

There is a particular academic depth to powerful knowledge. I have tried to articulate this profundity and rigour for Religious Education through these five concept-centred principles. I believe that powerful knowledge provides a strong conceptual platform for rigorous discipline-based discovery that, once mastered, transcends its own discipline-base to dialogue with powerful knowledge from other disciplines, and which itself becomes a creative intellectual impulse that can lead to the possibility of human progress. For Religious Education, powerful knowledge constitutes the *concepts that unlock a greater understanding* of the world; of the religions of the people who inhabit it; of human cultures and societies; of beliefs and values; of language and text; and of interpretation and thought. That is the reason why we need to talk about knowledge in RE.

References

All Party Parliamentary Group on RE (2013) *RE: The Truth Unmasked*. Accessed on 25 May 2017 at http://religiouseducationcouncil.org.uk/media/file/APPG_RE_-_The_Truth_Unmasked.pdf

All Party Parliamentary Group on RE (2014) *RE and Good Community Relations*. Accessed on 26 May 2017 from http://religiouseducationcouncil.org.uk/media/file/APPG_report_RE_and_good_community_re.pdf

Ball, S. (2006) Chapter 8: 'Educational Reform, Market Concepts and Ethical Re-tooling.' *Educational Policy and Social Class: The Selected Works of Stephen J. Ball.* London: Routledge.

Beck, J. (2008) *Meritocracy, Citizenship and Education: New Labour's Legacy.* London: Continuum.

Bhaskar, R. (2010) *Reclaiming Reality: A Critical Introduction to Contemporary Philosophy.* London: Taylor & Francis.

Earl, M. (2015) *RE-framing Education about Beliefs and Practices in Schools: A Lens and Tools (Concept Based) Approach.* University of Cambridge/Woolf Institute. Accessed on 26 May 2017 at www.woolf.cam.ac.uk/uploads/EducationProjectReport.pdf

Gibb, N. (2015) 'How E.D. Hirsch Came to Shape UK Government Policy.' In J. Simons and N. Porter (eds) *Knowledge and the Curriculum: A Collection of Essays to Accompany E.D. Hirsch's Lecture at Policy Exchange.* London: Policy Exchange.

Grimmitt, M. (2000) 'Contemporary Pedagogies of Religious Education: What Are They?' In M. Grimmitt (ed.) *Pedagogies of Religious Education* (pp.24–52). Great Wakering, Essex: McCrimmons.

Haydn, T. (2010) 'Secondary History.' In I. Davies (ed.) *Debates in Teaching History.* London: Routledge.

Hirsch, E.D., Jr (1987) *Cultural Literacy: What Every American Needs to Know.* Boston: Houghton Mifflin.

Kueh, R. (2014) *Revisiting the Rationale for Religious Education: Curriculum, Rigour and Powerful Knowledge.* Farmington Fellowship Report TT332. Available via www.farmington.ac.uk/index.php/tt332-revisiting-the-rationale-for-religious-education

Long, R. and Bolton, P. (2017) *English Baccalaureate.* House of Commons Briefing Paper SN06045. Accessed on 26 May 2017 at http://dera.ioe.ac.uk/28828/1/SN06045.pdf

Marx, K. (1926) *The Eighteenth Brumaire of Louis Bonaparte* (E. and C. Paul, transl.). London: George Allen & Unwin. (Original work published 1852.)

Nussbaum, M. (2010) *Not for Profit: Why Democracy Needs the Humanities.* Princeton, NJ: Princeton University Press.

Putnam, R. (2000) *Bowling Alone: The Collapse and Revival of American Community.* New York, NY: Simon and Schuster.

Religious Education Council (2013) *A Review of Religious Education in England.* London: RE Council.

White, J. (2007) 'What schools are for and why.' *Impact* No.14. Philosophy of Education Society of Great Britain. Accessed on 26 May 2017 at http://onlinelibrary.wiley.com/doi/10.1111/j.2048-416X.2007.tb00116.x/epdf

Wright, A. (2015) *Religious Education and Critical Realism: Knowledge, Reality and Religious Literacy.* London: Routledge.

Young, M. (2009) 'What Are Schools For?' In H. Daniels, H. Lauder and J. Porter (eds) *Knowledge, Values and Education Policy* (pp.10–18). London: Routledge.

Young, M. (2010) 'The future of education in a knowledge society: The radical case for a subject-based curriculum.' *Journal of the Pacific Circle Consortium for Education 22*, 1, 21–32.

Young, M. (2011) 'The return to subjects: A sociological perspective on the UK Coalition Government's approach to the 14–19 curriculum.' *The Curriculum Journal 22*, 2, 265–278.

Young, M. (2014) 'The Progressive Case for a Subject-based Curriculum.' In M. Young, D. Lambert, C. Roberts and M. Roberts (eds) *Knowledge and the Future School: Curriculum and Social Justice*. London: Bloomsbury.

Young, M. and Muller, J. (2010) 'Three educational scenarios for the future: Lessons from the sociology of knowledge.' *European Journal of Education 45*, 1, 11–27.

Chapter 4

WHY WE NEED LEGISLATIVE CHANGE, AND HOW WE CAN GET IT

MARK CHATER

Religious Education is sometimes brilliantly taught, and is essential to the curriculum; but its quality is too often undermined by legal and policy factors. The RE community cannot allow these factors to continue damaging the subject's quality: we need bold and positive change. This chapter begins by envisioning a better future, as a way of highlighting our current deficiencies; then I explain how the legal and policy factors, though unseen by many RE teachers, create handicaps for them all. Following this, a manifesto for a historic new legal basis tries to celebrate what is best about our current arrangements, while moving on beyond those aspects that weaken our subject's effectiveness or compromise its integrity. The views here are my own, but deeply influenced by conversations with hundreds of colleagues, and particularly the series of RE Thinking Days, which brought together some twenty-five leading practitioners in 2015–16 to grapple with the future models of RE.

The future and how we might get there

Let us travel forward in time to imagine the Ofsted survey report on RE in 2020. It reports that RE is an entitlement for all pupils without exception up to 16, parents having accepted the purpose and nature of RE and seeing no need to withdraw their children; that seven out of ten headteachers are clear about the core purpose of RE and show how they support it as a subject discipline; that most primary and secondary schools have a rigorous RE programme which fulfils their legal or contractual obligations; that teaching is usually good or outstanding, based on a clear progression pathway; that most primary and secondary teachers of RE know where to look for support, professional development and research opportunities; and that voluntary, inclusive local bodies help to resource RE within a framework of national expectations.

The first point to note about this vision is that it is a description of teachers, schools and school leaders. My start and end point in this argument is what happens in schools. Local and national bodies, statutory documents and professional or religious organisations are less important to me than schools. Anything that weakens, inhibits or prevents excellent RE in schools should be changed. From schools, I draw a connecting thread through documents, legal provisions and structures to show how the current legal and policy arrangements do damage to RE. The thread may be invisible to many RE teachers, but it still trips them up. In this chapter I hope to make the thread visible.

It might help to reflect on what aspects of the vision strike us as different from the present. This can lead us to an accurate diagnosis of the ways in which RE's current legal and policy arrangements are presenting obstacles to the kind of excellence, growth and consensus described above.

Chief among the differences is clarity of purpose. RE has no stated purpose in educational law. However, in its statutory local Agreed Syllabuses it currently has somewhere around five different aims. Depending on where you look, RE might be any or all of the following:

- An academic study of religion in one tradition or group of traditions (theology)

- An academic study of religion in general (religious studies)

- An academic study of philosophical and ethical problems, with reference to some religious and philosophical systems

- An instrumentalist project to promote attitudes of respect, tolerance, community cohesion or British values

- A personal development programme to explore spirituality, personal beliefs, ethical issues and (sometimes) personal, social and health education.

Any and each of those five is a fine thing to have in the curriculum. The problem comes when RE tries to do several or all of them at once. This creates an incoherent and scattergun curriculum that looks weak or desperate to chase relevance, and is composed of too many disciplines to be able to construct a progression pathway. This problem was reported as widespread and increasing in Ofsted 2013. Inspectors found that the subject was 'increasingly losing touch with the idea that RE should be primarily concerned with helping pupils to make sense of the world of religion and belief' (Ofsted 2013, p.14). Compounding this is the observation that RE's boundaries with other subjects such as citizenship and personal, social and health education are too weak and confused, so that RE is 'colonised' (Dinham and Shaw 2015, p.3).

Many of RE's constituent disciplines are historically in conflict with each other. For example, religious studies is an enlightenment idea whose original purpose was to break the controlling intellectual position of theology. As a social science, religious studies can create distance from truth claims, challenge notions of divine revelation or intervention as inconsistent with other forms of knowledge, and problematise religions as obstacles to progress (Gearon 2014). Spirituality, in its contemporary alternative sense, performs the function of offering people some alternatives to religion. It weaves forms of discipline, meaning and identity that may often borrow from religion but always eschew any connection with religious organisations or systems of thought (Heelas and Woodhead 2005). Since the intellectual and emotional rules of engagement are so radically different in theology, religious studies and spirituality, there can be no sense in which teachers or pupils have firm ground on which to pursue continuity and depth. A school subject that attempts to straddle these conflicts without acknowledging them, let alone resolving them, is avoiding the largest and hardest questions of all. Ambiguity, avoidance and suppressed contestation are built into the foundation of RE.

When the epistemological basis of the subject demonstrates this much confusion, the difficulties in requiring compliance or consent are magnified. The law requires schools to teach RE but has nothing clear to say about why. In an age less deferential than the 1940s or even the 1980s, this vagueness invites scepticism as to the value and viability of the endeavour.

Our next point of difference between vision and current reality concerns the content of RE. The vision speaks of a rigorous RE programme in schools, characterised by a clear progression pathway. Currently this is a problem of breadth and depth. The curriculum in many non-denominational schools has insufficient depth, continuity and coherence, resulting in low standards and superficial knowledge (Ofsted 2013). The learning experience is confusing, progression is unclear, and any aspiration to promote religious literacy is sabotaged from within. The prioritising of breadth in RE is usually a well-intentioned attempt to make RE part of an instrumentalist project to promote tolerance and respect. However, studying three or more religions or worldviews in a key stage creates major design challenges. How will the pupils accommodate their newly acquired knowledge? Is there a natural sequence whereby some religions or worldviews are more complex and rich, and therefore more challenging? Is there a risk that a broad RE curriculum, composed of one religion or worldview after another, makes progression impossible? Is there also a risk that insufficient time is devoted to exploring complexity, ambiguity and variety within each system of thought? Might this eventually result in superficial understanding, rather than literacy?

Meanwhile, concerns about RE in some schools with a religious character remain a point of controversy. At a philosophical level, some dispute the compatibility of religious nurture with liberal education (Best 2014). The narrowness of RE in some (not all) of these schools occasionally causes grave concern (Lichten 2014), though other investigations find no basis for the concerns (Oldfield, Hartnett and Bailey 2013). There is a suspicion that some bad practice, occasionally amounting to promoting exclusivism and contempt, is being kept from public view by religious inspection arrangements. This is becoming a matter of public debate (Clarke and Woodhead 2015; Wintour 2014). To some extent these difficulties can be addressed through professional development, discussion and soft influence. But the transparency required to provide reassurance can only be brought about through legal reform of RE's curriculum and inspection arrangements.

To round up the list of differences between vision and reality, we must mention the current rules on RE, which are so complicated that Heads, governors and even civil servants can get them wrong. RE is statutory but not National Curriculum; compulsory, but a parent can withdraw their child; determined by different rules and documents in at least eight different types of school; and generated by up to 151 local syllabuses, all broadly similar in content, but in form and structure so different and complex that it takes an army of advisers and consultants to interpret them. The system of Standing Advisory Councils on RE (SACREs) supporting local authorities and local syllabuses lacks the capacity and effectiveness to provide improvement for RE (All Party Parliamentary Group on RE 2013; Ofsted 2013), while 'many agreed syllabuses and guidance did not provide effective models of curriculum planning' (Ofsted 2013, p.13).

The hidden thread carries confusion and under-performance from policy to classroom. Its damage to RE is pedagogical, epistemological, curricular, structural – and fatal. To survive, RE needs a wholesale review and a new policy and legal basis.

Policy change or legal reform?

There is an alternative diagnosis still offered by some in the RE world and in wide circulation on social media, and it is this: RE is a great subject; its variety of purposes is a creative strength, not a weakness; meddling with the basic law on RE might result in something far worse; if the government would just recognise the great work RE does, all would be well. For example, this diagnosis calls on the government to include GCSE Religious Studies in the English Baccalaureate, enforce the law through inspections, affirm the work of SACREs and require providers of initial teacher training to guarantee some minimum time for RE. This is essentially a call for policy change, not legal reform. Sometimes, the diagnosis also proposes rescinding the parental right to withdraw. Since this alternative view is in wide circulation, it merits some critical discussion.

First, an argument for policy change alone is a 'business as usual' view that fails to dig deeply enough into the roots of RE's weakness, evidenced above. The policy changes asked for would mostly be desirable, although there is some debate about the advisability of becoming part of the English Baccalaureate. However, while such changes may be necessary, they are not sufficient. To stop and rest at that point would be to adopt a Pollyanna view of RE, overlooking the inspection evidence of muddled purposes and ignoring the recommendations in subsequent reports (Clarke and Woodhead 2015; Commission on Religion and Belief in British Public Life 2015; Dinham and Shaw 2015). If a model has been shown to produce failure, why should it be rewarded and reinforced? Change may be hard for some professionals in RE who have made their careers within the current system: they have derived their professional self-understanding, status and income from the current arrangements for syllabus-writing. To accept that change might be necessary requires a shift that is cognitively and emotionally challenging. Those who adhere to the 'business as usual' diagnosis, but additionally call for the right to withdraw to be rescinded, must explain how the state can require parents to surrender their freedom to withdraw when the state has not declared in statute what RE is for and what content it must or may include.

Second, the policy changes asked for run against the clear grain of political parties' thinking on education. Conservative politicians instinctively favour smaller government, de-regulation and innovation. Since 2010, Conservative govern-ments have had a mandate to convert local authority schools into academies and to create new Free Schools, to involve universities and independent schools, and to limit the role of local authorities (Conservative Party 2015, 2017). Labour's thinking (2017) is interested in school accountability but holds back from intervening in curriculum matters. From both parties there is a clear focus on school Heads as autonomous agents of change and improvement. To ask of any government that they reinforce laws and regulations on behalf of local authorities, issue directives to Heads, add further directives to a widening market of teacher-training providers, and affirm or even extend the writ of local Agreed Syllabuses is to ask them to ignore their philosophy and the policy on which they campaigned and won elections. It is to reinforce RE's exceptionalism, one of its greatest weaknesses.

So we may conclude that the diagnosis of policy reform alone is both insufficient to address RE's long-standing weaknesses, and highly unlikely to succeed even on its own limited terms. There is a need for increasing numbers of teachers, advisers, academics, Heads and policy makers to recognise that policy change and legal reform for RE must go hand in hand.

The legal impasse and how we can break it

At the heart of our impasse is the provision in the Education Reform Act 1988, repeated in the Education Act 1996, Section 375(3) and the School Standards and Framework Act 1998 Schedule 19(5) and subsequent Acts. The wording has not changed. Many RE professionals can quote it from memory:

> Agreed syllabuses must reflect the fact that religious traditions in Great Britain are in the main Christian, whilst taking account of the teaching and practices of the other principal religions represented in Great Britain. (Education Reform Act 1988, Section 8(3))

As a profession, our reasons for needing to change this law are multiple, so first some critical commentary is necessary.

The system of Agreed Syllabuses is collapsing as many and perhaps all local authority schools convert to academy status, becoming publicly funded schools outwith a local authority's orbit. The system, sometimes referred to as local determination, was showing signs of strain at the time of the last three Ofsted survey reports (Ofsted 2007, 2010, 2013). The factors that made it vulnerable then have accelerated since (Clarke and Woodhead 2015). Individual syllabuses can be good, but the Agreed Syllabus system, producing up to 151 versions of broadly the same content, is phenomenally wasteful and introduces unfortunate variances in quality. The legal requirements governing the way syllabuses are composed gives 50 percent of the representation to religious groups (Department for Children, Schools and Families 2010). This level of control by religious groups, whose *raison d'être* is their own representation in a positive light, is educationally inappropriate. It often results in arguments at local and national level about how much time should be given to one religion or another. These decisions should be given to professional teachers and curriculum designers, operating within national requirements. It is this inability of RE to liberate itself from religious control that gives it a lingering aura of something it so often wishes to disavow – confessionalism. Rather than shoring up a system that fits neither the aspirations of schools and teachers, nor the pattern of school provision, we need a new law.

From time to time, the RE community debates the future of the Agreed Syllabus system, often with some feeling. The debate has tended to polarise 'local' and 'national', as if they were mutually exclusive. But RE is bigger than 'local or national'; we need to break this binary assumption. RE is global and national and local. Young people first engage with religion and belief as a global reality, brought to them through the media, and as a local encounter in their immediate community. Later in life they also engage with it as a facet of nationhood and identity (Commission on Religion and Belief in British Public Life 2015). RE is in need of a new settlement that reflects the best of global, national and truly local inputs. In the local/national debate, it is important that there be no losers. It may be that the solution could keep the best features of local RE while introducing a new national requirement on all publicly funded schools.

We should also raise questions about the language of the 1988 Act's provision for RE. For example, what does it mean for a statutory curriculum document to 'reflect' a fact? It is usually assumed to impose some quantitative rules on RE, such as a larger share for Christianity. However, this is speculative, and more precise requirements would be helpful. Why should the content of RE be reflected by religious demography ('religious traditions in Great Britain')? And why Great Britain solely? In 1988 we did not live in a globalised world; now we do. Religions and beliefs hold out the possibility of terrible threats and violence, and also the blessings of peace and understanding. These global patterns, negative and positive, affect this country. It is probable that most teachers would wish to see RE shaped by global, national and local patterns.

The Act's reference to Christianity places this religion in an increasingly vulnerable position. It is still reasonable to claim that Christianity has historically done more to shape this country than any other religious or philosophical position. But in a recent survey of British social attitudes, those self-identifying as having no religion – the 'nones' – emerge as the largest group (NatCen 2016). If the long-term decline of churchgoing numbers continues, we shall need a more robust basis for giving a central place to Christianity. One is suggested in the new legal wording below.

In a phrase that feels squirmingly condescending, the 1988 Act enjoins RE to 'take account of...other principal religions'. There has long been some fuzziness over what the 'principal' religions might be. I once heard Department for Education (DfE) lawyers opine that it must refer to the 'big six'. That opinion, if it were established in precedent, would leave the study of ancient and influential philosophies such as Zoroastrianism outside the law. But the point is that there is no clarity.

Next we come to the most egregious fault in the Act: the word 'religions'. The Human Rights Act 1998 requires laws that are incompatible with the European Convention on Human Rights (ECHR) to be reinterpreted to be compatible, if possible. Discrimination between the religious and the non-religious is forbidden under the ECHR. Thus even the present law, when reinterpreted, requires RE to 'take account of' non-religious worldviews, such as atheism, humanism or existentialism, as well as religious ones. But this reinterpretation is a clumsy instrument; a less convoluted measure is needed. In a Brexit Britain, the UK will still be a signatory to the Convention (Conservative Party 2017). Therefore there will still be a legal precedent, as well as a moral and educational case, for requiring RE to teach about religious and non-religious worldviews.

Summing up our discussion of the 1988 Act's underpinning of RE, we can say:

- The Agreed Syllabus system can no longer cater effectively as a basis for RE in all schools.

- The relationship between syllabuses and demographic patterns of religion, captured in the words 'reflect' and 'in Britain', is unsatisfactory.

- If Christianity ceases to be a majority religion in the UK, there are still historical and constitutional reasons for ensuring its place in the RE curriculum, and this should be given a more robust and less ambiguous basis.

- There can be no legal formula that excludes, or appears to exclude, religious or non-religious belief systems or philosophies of life from the RE curriculum.

The 1988 provision for RE is obsolete in one other respect, concerning our national harmony and security. Our country now faces a serious threat of global, organised religious violence and hatred on an unprecedented scale, as well as an upsurge of far-right groups very hostile to religious and cultural diversity (BBC News 2016). In both cases, hate speech, bullying, threats of violence and actual violence affect children and families in the UK. Both kinds of extremism thrive on ignorance, simplistic arguments and poor reasoning, sometimes described as low levels of religious literacy. In this charged and ominous context, we urgently need expectations on all publicly funded schools – expectations that are clear and unambiguous in promoting religious literacy. And we need inspection and accountability arrangements that more effectively guard against the promotion of extremism, for the protection of all communities. In turn, the inspection and accountability measures must, if they are to work at all, be based on a very clear legal requirement.

The foremost global project to study fundamentalism in its many forms (Marty and Appleby 2004) has exposed some recurrent characteristics of fundamentalism, among them concentrated power, simplistic use of texts and ahistorical, apocalyptic, binary moralities. We therefore need schools to teach the internal diversity, historical development, complexity and hermeneutic richness of religions. These features, though not always with these words, are built into the proposed new law below.

A new law

The new legal basis of RE needs to be consistent with the DfE's priorities for diverse kinds of maintained schools; it needs to reflect the nation's religious and cultural traditions and its modern realities in a globalised world. What follows is not intended to be a curriculum document, more a replacement for the 1988 clause quoted above. Curriculum documents, national and local, would be required to operate within this proposed law. Indeed, if this proposal or some version of it meets with agreement in the RE community, it might even create a way out of the national/local binary thinking. Any new legal basis of RE needs to be high-level, unambiguous, permissive where possible, prescriptive when necessary, and – above all – brief:

All publicly funded schools must deliver RE to every registered pupil in every year. School RE programmes must, as a minimum, be designed in accordance with the facts that:

- *Britain and the world are religiously and philosophically diverse.*

- *Christianity as a living, diverse and global faith is the main religion that has shaped British heritage and culture.*

- *Theological and philosophical ideas, traditions and ways of life are internally diverse and change over time.*

- *Religious and non-religious worldviews and identities can relate positively and negatively to current issues and events.*

- *Texts, ethical ideas and belief systems can be applied and interpreted in different ways.*

RE teaching must offer knowledge and understanding of Christianity and a range of other religions and world views, including those of local significance where appropriate. Teaching must promote respect, openness, scholarly accuracy, reasoning and critical enquiry.

There may be plenty to disagree with in this proposed new law; I look forward to critical comments and suggestions from readers. There remain several other important questions: about the name of the subject, the parental right to withdraw, the age range for which RE should be compulsory, the future of SACREs and Agreed Syllabuses, and the provision of initial and continuing professional development. But first let RE in all classrooms have a firm and fitting basis in law.

References

All Party Parliamentary Group on RE (2013) *RE: The Truth Unmasked*. Accessed on 25 May 2017 at http://religiouseducationcouncil.org.uk/media/file/APPG_RE_-_The_Truth_Unmasked.pdf

BBC News (2016, 13 October) 'Race and religious hate crimes rose 41% after EU vote.' Accessed on 27 May 2017 at www.bbc.co.uk/news/uk-politics-37640982

Best, R. (2014) 'Spirituality, Faith and Education: Some Reflections from a UK Perspective'. In J. Watson, M. de Souza and A. Trousdale (eds) *Global Perspectives on Spirituality and Education* (pp.5–20). New York and Abingdon: Routledge.

Clarke, C. and Woodhead, L. (2015) *A New Settlement: Religion and Belief in Schools*. Lancaster University: Westminster Faith Debates. Accessed on 25 May 2017 at http://faithdebates.org.uk/wp-content/uploads/2015/06/A-New-Settlement-for-Religion-and-Belief-in-schools.pdf

Commission on Religion and Belief in British Public Life (2015) *Living with Difference: Community, Diversity and the Common Good*. Accessed on 25 May 2017 at www.woolf.cam.ac.uk/uploads/LivingwithDifference.pdf

Conservative Party (2015) *The Conservative Party Manifesto*. Accessed on 27 May 2017 at www.bond.org.uk/data/files/Blog/ConservativeManifesto2015.pdf

Conservative Party (2017) *Forward, Together: The Conservative Manifesto*. Accessed on 27 May 2017 at https://s3.eu-west-2.amazonaws.com/manifesto2017/Manifesto2017.pdf

Department for Children, Schools and Families (2010) *Religious Education in English Schools: Non-statutory Guidance*. London: DCSF.

Dinham, A. and Shaw, M. (2015) *RE for Real: The Future of Teaching and Learning About Religion and Belief*. London: Goldsmiths University.

Gearon, L. (2014) *On Holy Ground: The Theory and Practice of Religious Education*. Abingdon: Routledge.

Heelas, P. and Woodhead, L. (2005) *The Spiritual Revolution: Why Religion is Giving Way to Spirituality*. Oxford: Blackwell.

Labour Party (2017) *For the Many not the Few: The Labour Party Manifesto 2017*. London: Labour Party. Accessed on 29 May 2017 at www.labour.org.uk/index.php/manifesto2017

Lichten, A. (2014, 23 September) 'A contested subject: RE and faith schools' [Blog post]. National Secular Society. Accessed on 27 May 2017 at www.secularism.org.uk/blog/2014/09/a-contested-subject--religious-education-and-faith-schools

Marty, M. and Appleby, S. (2004) *Accounting for Fundamentalisms: The Dynamic Character of Movements*. Chicago, IL: Chicago University Press.

NatCen (2016) *British Social Attitudes*. London: NatCen. Accessed on 25 June 2017 at www.natcen.ac.uk/our-research/research/british-social-attitudes

Ofsted (2007) *Making Sense of Religion*. London: Ofsted.

Ofsted (2010) *Transforming Religious Education*. London: Ofsted.

Ofsted (2013) *Religious Education: Realising the Potential*. Accessed on 25 May 2017 at www.gov.uk/government/publications/religious-education-realising-the-potential

Oldfield, E., Hartnett, L. and Bailey, E. (2013) *More Than an Educated Guess: Assessing the Evidence on Faith Schools*. London: Theos.

Wintour, P. (2014, 29 October) 'Ofsted should inspect religious teaching in faith schools, says Tristram Hunt.' *The Guardian*. Accessed on 27 May 2017 at www.theguardian.com/education/2014/oct/29/ofsted-inspect-religious-education-faith-schools-tristram-hunt

Chapter 5

THE FUTURE OF CATHOLIC RELIGIOUS EDUCATION IN THE CONTEXT OF PROPOSED WIDER REFORM

ANDREW LEWIS

This chapter begins by briefly exploring the history of RE in Catholic schools as a context within which its distinctiveness will be defined and is best understood. Then I explore how the Catholic vision of good RE fits within the broader vision of RE held by the RE community as a whole in England, arguing that RE from a religious perspective brings an important breadth to what has always been a pluralistic discipline. Following from that, I look at the current contested areas within RE and consider how the Catholic RE community might respond to these threats and challenges, while spelling out those areas that would be non-negotiables beyond which Catholic RE could not pass without losing its authenticity. With all of this in mind, the chapter concludes by considering some possible futures for Catholic RE. In this section I argue for the importance for pupils in all schools of a study of religion that allows a deep theological engagement with at least one tradition, as is exemplified by Catholic RE. Such an engagement is the only one that allows for a proper grasp of historicity, nuance and complexity, all of which are essential skills in navigating a world of simplistic religious extremes.

The story of the Catholic commitment to education

Catholic education has an ambitious vision of human potential, most recently proclaimed by the present pope:

> A school's mission is to develop the sense of the true, the sense of the good, the sense of the beautiful. (Pope Francis 2014)

The Catholic Church was the first provider of schools and universities in England, with cathedral and monastic schools established from the late sixth century onwards. During the Reformation, these schools were either re-founded by the Church of England or forced abroad or underground.

Catholic schools began to return to England in the late 1700s and early 1800s. In 1847, the state and the Catholic Poor-School Committee agreed to the opening of Catholic primary schools, following the first Anglican schools that began from around 1811 onwards. After the restoration of the Catholic hierarchy in 1850, the Bishops decided the priority was to build schools first, and church buildings later; this highlighted the fundamental importance of Catholic education. A school building programme continued well into the 20th century, with a priority for serving the poor, hence the high numbers of Catholic schools in less affluent areas.

The 1944 Education Act saw the majority of Catholic schools becoming Voluntary Aided, with state funding. The first Catholic academy opened in 2005, and since 2011 many have become academy converters. This partnership between the Church and State was one the Church entered into gradually and with certain provisos. Among the conditions of the partnership, one very important agreement then and now was that the Bishops of England and Wales would continue to have jurisdiction over the curriculum and inspection of Religious Education. The land and buildings of the school are often still owned by the Church, but running costs are shared by government and Church. The statutory protections for maintained Catholic schools were replicated in each of the funding agreements for the new Catholic academies. Today, the Catholic Church currently educates over 800,000 pupils and students in over 2000 schools, which is 10 percent of all schools (Catholic Education Service 2014).

Catholic schools are a legacy of the commitment and sacrifice of generations to a vision of Catholic education. That commitment was and is founded both on a belief that education is wholly valuable and a key to social advancement and betterment, and on an equally important conviction that the Catholic tradition offers something worth preserving, studying and contributing to. To understand why Catholic schools were founded, what the founders hoped to preserve and what the future holds can help us better understand what makes the schools distinctive.

Catholic RE's distinctiveness and its critics

Pope Benedict XVI (2010) summarised extensive Vatican documents on education by emphasising a rounded education as a fundamental motivation behind the work of Catholic schools. There is a clear emphasis on the students, rather than simply a subject like any other in the school curriculum. This is exactly what is meant when schools refer to the education of the whole person.

No education can be value-free or neutral; there is always a hidden curriculum, a set of values that students within a school are expected to conform to. All teaching and learning involves the transmission of values, and Catholic education has a considered set of values that make it distinctive. The Catholic essayist and apologist G.K. Chesterton pointed out the danger of pretending that education can be value-free:

> Every education teaches a philosophy; if not by dogma then by suggestion, by implication, by atmosphere. Every part of that education has a connection with every other part. If it does

not all combine to convey some general view of life, it is not education at all. (Chesterton 1950, p.167)

Religious Education in Catholic schools does have dual meaning, both as something that permeates all aspects of school life, and as a distinct subject discipline. These two aspects cannot be disconnected. The acquiring of knowledge goes hand in hand with growing in wisdom (Congregation for Catholic Education 1997). The subject discipline of Religious Education usually fills 10 percent of the curriculum time; it is both distinctive and inclusive. The *Curriculum Directory* makes clear that Religious Education must be academic for all, whilst its outcomes and relevance will vary for some:

> Religious Education in schools should be regarded as an academic discipline with the same systematic demands and the same rigour as other disciplines. For some...Religious Education will also be received as evangelisation and for some, catechesis. (Catholic Bishops' Conference of England and Wales 2012, p.3)

It is vital to remember that catechesis (continuing formation in faith) does remain a separate, distinct activity:

> Religious education is different from, and complementary to, catechesis, as it is school education that does not require the assent of faith, but conveys knowledge on the identity of Christianity and Christian life. Moreover, it enriches the Church and humanity with areas for growth, of both culture and humanity. (Congregation for Catholic Education 2009, n.18)

Overall, the aim and mission of the Catholic school is 'to form strong and responsible individuals, who are capable of making free and correct choices' (Sacred Congregation for Religious Education 1977, n.31). The whole curriculum must be driven by the values found in the Gospels: respect for life, love, solidarity, truth and justice. Yet this must not be confused with the academic pursuits of Religious Education, which has as its aim a secure knowledge and understanding of the Catholic theological tradition.

Some claim there are fundamental pedagogical differences in Catholic RE; the terms 'confessional' or 'faith nurture' are often applied. Critics claim that RE becomes simply a form of indoctrination, even proselytising. Yet pedagogy in RE as a whole is contentious: some favour a phenomenological approach, others prefer a more human-developmental approach or a critical-realist model. It is at times hard to identify what form of criticism is being applied: it may be content-related, whereby Catholic RE has a clear focus on Catholic Christianity and scripture, or it may be a linguistic criticism, whereby teachers may talk about 'our beliefs' rather than 'Catholics believe'. Catholic schools have a huge variety of intake, and it would be impossible to make generalisations. While parents retain the role as primary and principal educators, the family is the primary, but not the only and exclusive, educating community (Pope John Paul II 1981). Parents, in general, choose a Catholic school either actively to support their child's faith, or with the understanding that the Catholic faith will be a key feature of their child's education.

Some critics claim that the term *theology* is something that can solely be used to describe a process that happens inside a faith community. This criticism argues that Catholic RE is simply teaching for commitment, at best, and potentially proselytising. Many would be happy to agree that Catholic RE is teaching from a position of commitment; as such it is not a simple phenomenological approach.

Terence Copley (2008) points out the complexity of the term *confessionalism* and suggests that many non-faith schools now display a secular confessionalism in RE, whereby a form of indoctrination takes place into a different, often undefined, set of values. Copley raises the concern that if religious belief is simply a matter of private conscience and optional personal alliance, students are not fully aware of the truth claims being made by religions. Does RE become something sanitised, simply promoting tolerance and multi-culturalism? Religion can seem trivial if its claims are not engaged with seriously. Copley proposes a 'world-religions-plus-spirituality' approach, with a clear focus on people's sacred yearnings (2005, p.138). He suggests that a more confessional approach is appropriate, 'to nurture children in the heritage religion of their culture' while 'allowing them the freedom to discuss and question' (p.113). It can be argued easily that students need such an approach to fully understand what belief means to be faithful or what belonging to a religious community is like. This vision for RE would be common in Catholic schools, despite the negative connotations attached by some.

In a Catholic school, knowledge and understanding are far more than the accumulation of information. The schools aspire to teach love of wisdom, habituating each student to desire and delight in learning (Miller 2006).

Common ground in the relationship between Catholic RE and RE in other contexts

Who am I? Where have I come from and where am I going? Why is there evil? What is there after this life? To deny these questions is to deny our humanity.

Pope John Paul II 1998, p.1

Pope John Paul II made it clear that all humans were natural philosophers, something which is undoubtedly cultivated in RE classrooms everywhere, and is certainly not unique to the Catholic school. While in Catholic schools there is the aim to enable students to think with the Church (*sentire cum ecclesia*), students elsewhere need to think with something else. As Copley argued, this might be a set of secular values which may or may not be universally agreed, but is certainly part of the hidden curriculum in non-faith schools. Access to good quality RE is a necessary part of this, and it is the start point of agreement with the wider RE community.

What Catholic schools aim to teach is a 2000-year body of thought, literature and art that has been historically influential and continues to influence the 1.1 billion Catholics in the world today. It is significant religiously, culturally and historically. However, if Catholics are to understand their own tradition, they need to do so in dialogue with those who are not Catholic (Congregation for Catholic Education 2013). It is therefore important that a broad curriculum of belief and non-belief is studied.

While Catholic schools are under the direction of their own diocesan Bishops, there is no reason to not support the wider RE community. Catholic schools share in many of the same issues facing community schools; there is variation in the quality of teaching, and teacher shortages are shared. However, they often have the benefits of a larger RE team, greater access to resources, more time and a higher profile within the school.

The majority of Catholic schools spend approximately half a term per year studying a different religion. Despite being proportionately less than community schools, it is often comparable in teaching hours: for example with two hours per week, half a term's study would mean approximately 16 hours of teaching. Units on Islam, Judaism and Hinduism would often be comparable to community schools. It would therefore often make sense for greater collaboration with the wider RE community to ensure accurate, academic teaching of these other religions.

A significant number of Catholic students do not attend Catholic schools. This makes it important for the Church to ensure, in so far as it can, that Catholicism is taught accurately in community schools. A renewed emphasis in the 2016 GCSE syllabuses on diversity with traditions means that the Catholic view is often cited. Dialogue between schools, and RE teachers, would be mutually helpful for all.

Religious Education remains a diverse subject, with many interested parties; yet it is clear that Catholic RE shares a universal calling to the love of wisdom and passion for truth. The Catholic intellectual tradition cherishes, develops and employs a valuable treasury of texts that are considered worth preserving. These are written texts, musical texts, art, customs and rituals, and modes of thought, expression and action. They are finished products that need to remain in high status, and be studied and understood. The Catholic intellectual tradition is committed to introducing students to these texts.

Additionally, many Catholic schools are trying to create clear distinctions between RE and liturgy. In the same way, many RE teachers in community schools are attempting to remove collective worship from being the sole responsibility of the RE department.

Points of principle and points of debate in current Catholic RE

As this chapter is being written, the Commission on Religious Education is asking for evidence to be submitted on the future of RE. The Commission's first question is: What are the main aims and purposes of Religious Education? This question cuts straight to the heart of the difficulty that the RE profession faces, since the disagreements about the answer to the question do not fall neatly along the lines one might expect; there is just as much disagreement between those who would consider the RE they teach to be non-confessional as there is between these professionals and those in Catholic schools.

It might be helpful to lay out some of these points of tension before exploring where Catholic RE sits within them. One tension is between the affective and the cognitive; between a vision of RE as some sort of personal development like personal, social and health education, citizenship or sex education, as distinct from a vision of RE as a serious academic study with its own body of knowledge to be mastered. A second tension is that between thematic and systematic approaches to curriculum design; between studies that seek to explore the big questions from the multiple religion and belief perspectives, and those that seek to understand the coherence of one religion at a time, in order to understand how the different parts of it are connected to each other. A third tension is between RE as a broad study of religions and beliefs, giving equal weight to each, and a focus in depth on one religion. This latter position could mean the study of only one religion, or it could mean privileging one religion in terms of the proportion of curriculum time spent studying it, while referring to some others. Finally, there is the tension between religion viewed from the outside (focusing on religious belief as a sociological category, asking questions about why humans are religious, and trying to discover underlying sociological or psychological reasons for religious belief and behaviours) and studying religion from the inside (focusing on how a religion understands itself, studying the questions that a particular religion considers to be of importance). Of course, with each of these tensions, one does not have to choose exclusively one pole or the other; it is possible for one and the same RE curriculum to be at different points on each of these spectrums at different times. Still, there are clearly those who are advocating a shift to one or other sides of each of these polarities. The Catholic community is keen to play its part in this ongoing conversation, since its own position is in a state of development.

It is no doubt true that there was once a time when the religious instruction in the classroom was merely an extension of the catechesis received in the home and in the parish. In some respects, the term 'catechesis' is unique in Catholic discussions about RE, or at least more prominent than it is in other settings. Franchi (2016, p.18) gives a succinct and helpful definition: 'Catechesis is the term traditionally used to describe the ongoing faith formation of the baptised.' In addition to signifying to whom and to what end religious instruction is given, the term has also come to refer to a particular pedagogical approach. Catechetical approaches to religious learning, because they are intended to bring about growth in faith and personal commitment, have focused on pedagogies that are child-centred. These pedagogies have tended to sacrifice systematic rigour for the sake of personal engagement. They can sometimes be more concerned with attracting students to the faith than with teaching them about it. A catechetical approach to RE, therefore, in terms of the tensions set out previously, would emphasise the affective over the cognitive, the systematic over the thematic, depth over breadth and theology over sociology.

In a context where Catholic schools were genuinely an extension of the home and parish – where every member of staff and every pupil was a practising Catholic – it was almost natural that RE would be some form of catechesis, as laid out above. But Catholic schools have changed somewhat since their foundation in the latter half of the 19th century. They are now among the most ethnically and socially diverse schools in the country. They are religiously diverse too. The most recent survey of Catholic schools in England and Wales carried out by the Catholic Education Service (2014) found that Catholic schools contain a rich mix of Catholics, other Christians, Muslims, Jews, Hindus, Sikhs, Buddhists and a large minority of pupils who self-identify as non-religious. Catholic primary schools were more ethnically diverse than the national average. In such a context, new thinking about RE and its relationship to catechesis was inevitable.

The development of Catholic ideas was not only a response to shifts in demography, but was more a reflection of a profound series of reflections that were happening in Rome at the same time. The first of these was the shift in the attitude of the Church to other religions, following from the groundwork laid during the Second Vatican Council. In the most recent expression of this thinking, it is clear that education in Catholic schools 'must take into account the growing multi-religious component of society, with the consequent need to know about different beliefs and dialogue both with those beliefs and with non-believers' (Congregation for Catholic Education 2013, p.55). And this engagement is not presented by the document in a spirit of reluctance but is seen as a positive expression of the Catholic vision of education that seeks the full participation of every member of the school community. Such participation 'flourishes in a climate of dialogue and mutual respect, in an educational setting where all are assured of being able to increase their capacities to the full, with the constant aim of pursuing the good of all' (p.56).

So in terms of the breadth/depth polarity, it should be clear that Catholic RE will always include the teaching of other religions and beliefs. As has already been said, it is probably the case that although the proportion of curriculum time spent teaching other religions may be smaller than in other schools, the actual time in hours is probably greater; it is likely to be approaching something like 17–20 hours per year, at least half a school year in many community schools. So whilst in Catholic schools, greater prominence will be given to the teaching of Catholicism, this depth will not be at the expense of breadth.

RE's subject content is to be approached with the same serious and critical openness as the study of any academic subject on the curriculum (Franchi 2016). Whilst there is a clear distinction between RE and catechesis, the RE curriculum is ultimately at the service of the catechetical mission of the school. That is, the Catholic school is a community of faith, where those who are not of that faith are invited to live with and alongside it and those who are of the faith are invited to immerse themselves more deeply in its richness.

So, if RE is not catechesis, in what sense does it serve the larger catechetical mission of the school? In this sense: RE is the place where Catholics gain greater knowledge and understanding of their faith through a critical and systematic engagement with the Catholic theological tradition to which they, through their baptism, belong.

This combination of depth and breadth, a curriculum that majors in one religious tradition without neglecting the others, has advantages that the broad but superficial alternatives lack. These advantages need not be exclusive to Catholic RE, since the combination of depth in one religion with breadth in the others leads to something much more substantial than mere religious literacy, and approaches something more like religious mastery. This will be explored briefly in the final section of this chapter.

However, before we leave this section, it is important to discuss where Catholic schools may stand in response to the recommendations in the interim report of the Commission on RE, due in Autumn 2017. If the Commission were to recommend a common baseline entitlement for all schools, including schools with a religious character, then it is very likely that the RE curricula of Catholic schools would already be in compliance with it. But since one of the conditions of the partnership between Church and State is the right of the Bishops to set the curriculum in Catholic schools, then any statutory imposition of just such a common baseline is potentially highly problematic. Of course, given what has already been said, this will only be a problem in principle, not in practice. Nonetheless, the principle is a fundamental and non-negotiable one for the Catholic Church in England. It is hoped that a way forward can be found that ensures outstanding Religious Education for all without backing the Bishops into a corner where they have no option but to oppose something that, in every detail but one, they would otherwise welcome and support.

Religious literacy is not enough

Currently there is much discussion of the importance of religious literacy. Alan Brine, former subject specialist adviser for RE to Ofsted, finds its lack worrying (Ofsted 2013). Similarly Clarke and Woodhead (2015) commented on weaknesses in developing religious literacy in schools at a time when it is more sorely needed than ever. It is no less important to the Catholic Bishops of England and Wales, who are unequivocal about its centrality (Catholic Bishops' Conference 2012).

Yet 'literacy' is the term we generally reserve for basic grasp of material – from the kind of study that secures competence but not excellence. This is insufficient for the sake of achieving the larger goals for which religious literacy is usually proffered as the panacea. What is needed is expertise, not just literacy. The kind of combination of depth and breadth that characterises the Catholic approach to RE will serve as a much better preparation for living well with our diverse neighbours.

The sociologist of religion Grace Davie notes with alarm the decline in religious literacy, including among people of a secular outlook:

> British people are losing their knowledge of religion (that is, of vocabulary, concept and narrative) just when they need this most, given the requirement, on an increasingly regular basis, to pass judgement on the rights and obligations of the very varied religious actors (individual and corporate) that currently cohabit in this country. The consequent debates all too often are both ill informed and ill mannered, as questions that were considered closed are not only re-opened, but are also engaged with little or no preparation. (Davie 2015, pp.ix–x)

It is perhaps also worth wondering why extremist forms of religious commitment have arisen at the same time as the RE curriculum has become broader in its coverage of religions. Could it be that knowing less about more has led to a decline in the ability of young people to think clearly and well about religion? Franchi (2016) thinks there may well be a connection, in the form of the removal of the conceptual and linguistic resources needed to think critically in the face of ideologies. This is speculative of course, but it suggests how an emphasis on breadth at the expense of depth could be connected to these multiple ways in which as a culture we have failed to achieve even the most basic forms of religious literacy.

The thought is this: If we spend the relatively small amount of time we have for RE covering every one of the various manifestations of religion and belief that are common in the UK and the world, it is inevitable that a systematic study of any one of them is likely to be very difficult, if not impossible. Precisely by aiming for a broad religious literacy, what we actually achieve is perhaps a superficial understanding of the nature of any kind of religious commitment. But perhaps even worse than this, there is the possibility that students fail to realise that religions and religious belief are complex, nuanced, historically conditioned and internally diverse. Without this knowledge, they are liable to fall into two opposite sorts of trap: first, they may be misled into caricatures of religion in a way that leads to a dismissal of the religious perspective as trite, trivial or unthinking; second, they may become susceptible to totalising and extremist forms of religious narrative, since they lack the critical capacity to expose these perverted forms of religious belief to the scrutiny of a well-formed intellect. Thus a lack of expertise in one religion produces a failure of religious literacy in all. Again, this is speculative and no doubt in need of further research. However, the idea that becoming an expert in at least one tradition will lead to improved religious literacy overall is, if not obvious, then at least *prima facie* plausible.

References

Catholic Bishops' Conference of England and Wales (2012) *The Religious Education Curriculum Directory (3–19) for Catholic Schools and Colleges*. London: Catholic Bishops' Conference.

Catholic Education Service (2014) *Catholic Education in England and Wales*. London: CES. Accessed 27 May 2017 at www.catholiceducation.org.uk/images/CatholicEducationEnglandandWales.pdf

Chesterton, G.K. (1950) *The Common Man*. London: Sheed and Ward.

Clarke, C. and Woodhead, L. (2015) *A New Settlement: Religion and Belief in Schools*. Lancaster University: Westminster Faith Debates. Accessed on 25 May 2017 at http://faithdebates.org.uk/wp-content/uploads/2015/06/A-New-Settlement-for-Religion-and-Belief-in-schools.pdf

Congregation for Catholic Education (1997) *The Catholic School on the Threshold of the Third Millennium*. Rome: The Vatican. Accessed on 24 April 2017 at www.vatican.va/roman_curia/congregations/ccatheduc/documents/rc_con_ccatheduc_doc_27041998_school2000_en.html

Congregation for Catholic Education (2009) *Circular Letter to the Presidents of Bishops' Conferences on Religious Education in Schools*. Rome: The Vatican.

Accessed on 27 May 2017 at www.vatican.va/roman_curia/congregations/ccatheduc/documents/rc_con_ccatheduc_doc_20090505_circ-insegn-relig_en.html

Congregation for Catholic Education (2013) *Educating to Intercultural Dialogue in Catholic Schools: Living in Harmony for a Civilization of Love*. Accessed on 27 May 2017 at www.vatican.va/roman_curia/congregations/ccatheduc/documents/rc_con_ccatheduc_doc_20131028_dialogo-interculturale_en.html#Presence_in_Schools

Copley, T. (2005) *Indoctrination, Education and God*. London: SPCK.

Copley, T. (2008) *Teaching Religion: Sixty Years of Religious Education in England and Wales*. Exeter: University of Exeter Press.

Davie, G. (2015) Foreword. In A. Dinham and M. Francis, *Religious Literacy in Policy and Practice* (pp vii–xi). Bristol: Policy Press.

Franchi, L. (2016) *Shared Mission: Religious Education in the Catholic Tradition*. London: Scepter.

Miller, J. (2006) *The Holy See's Teaching on Catholic Schools*. Manchester, NH: Sophia Institute Press.

Ofsted (2013) *Religious Education: Realising the Potential*. Accessed on 25 May 2017 at www.gov.uk/government/publications/religious-education-realising-the-potential

Pope Benedict XVI (2010) *Celebration of Catholic Education: Address of the Holy Father to Teachers and Religious*. Rome: The Vatican. Accessed on 27 May 2017 at https://w2.vatican.va/content/benedict-xvi/en/speeches/2010/september/documents/hf_ben-xvi_spe_20100917_mondo-educ.html

Pope Francis (2014) *Address of Pope Francis to Students and Teachers from across Italy*. Accessed on 27 May 2017 at https://w2.vatican.va/content/francesco/en/speeches/2014/may/documents/papa-francesco_20140510_mondo-della-scuola.html

Pope John Paul II (1981) *Familiaris Consortio (Apostolic Exhortation on the Role of the Christian Family in the Modern World)*. Rome: The Vatican. Accessed on 27 May 2017 at http://w2.vatican.va/content/john-paul-ii/en/apost_exhortations/documents/hf_jp-ii_exh_19811122_familiaris-consortio.html

Pope John Paul II (1998) *Fides et Ratio* [Faith and Reason]. Rome: The Vatican.

Sacred Congregation for Catholic Education (1977) *The Catholic School*. Rome: The Vatican.

Chapter 6

RE-DRESSING THE BALANCE

GILLIAN GEORGIOU AND KATHRYN WRIGHT

This chapter argues that the future and sustainability of RE depends upon an ability to provide a balanced framework for the subject. In the light of the most recent inspection survey of RE (Ofsted 2013) and the Church of England's analysis of RE in its schools (Church of England 2014), as well as our own professional experiences working with teachers, we identify the need to ensure that Religious Education maintains a balance between theology, philosophy and the human and social sciences.

The dangers of an unbalanced curriculum

Our own teaching experience, and our observations of others, indicate that children and young people currently experience two key fields of study in their RE lessons: philosophy (or perhaps more specifically philosophy of religion) and a selection of disciplines that we might broadly understand as the human and social sciences. In primary schools teaching is often seen to fit into the latter field of study: it involves learning about ways in which religious believers and faith communities *act*, with an emphasis on things like festivals, rites of passage, places of worship and rituals associated with worship. This creates an understanding of religion and belief that focuses on *human phenomena*: this person is a Muslim because they *do* this, that person is a Christian because they *wear* that.

What is rarely seen, however, is an approach that attempts to help children understand the rich internal diversity of religions and beliefs. We do not deny the importance of engaging with the human phenomena of religion and belief, but we are cautious of such phenomena being presented as though there were only one way of being Muslim, Christian, Sikh and so on. The inherent risk of this approach (the 'all Christians...' approach) is that our pupils come away with the impression that religions are monolithic objects, a picture that is not true to the lived reality of religion and belief throughout human history (Dinham and Shaw 2015; Jackson 1997). In addition, we often see an idealised view of the religion or belief presented, which bears little resemblance to reality. Even where diversity is acknowledged, there is a danger that religion is perceived predominantly in terms of its function, particularly in relation to social control, cohesion and personal identity. This approach tends to ignore the conceptual basis of religions and beliefs, particularly those concepts that relate to the supernatural.

In secondary schools, teaching in RE is more often approached within the general field of philosophy and, perhaps more specifically, the field of philosophy of religion. This is in no small part connected to the previous GCSE in Religious Studies, which heavily emphasised both philosophy of religion and ethical studies. Consequently, much of the secondary RE curriculum from Key Stage 3 onwards can be focused on an exploration of 'big ideas', 'big questions' and 'big issues' (Ofsted 2013). Such an approach creates an imbalance and discontinuity with primary RE. Many primary schools struggle to cover the breadth of religions and belief systems required by RE syllabuses; consequently, depth can be sacrificed. The assumption that the more appropriate focus at secondary level is philosophy and ethics suggests that young people cannot, or do not need to, deepen their understanding of religions and beliefs as they progress through school. It is certainly the case that students could achieve very high grades in the old GCSE Religious Studies without needing detailed and deep knowledge and understanding of religious beliefs and teachings. It is perhaps no surprise that secondary RE teachers have responded to this by delivering a curriculum that more heavily focuses on philosophy and ethics, teaching religious concepts only insofar as they relate to philosophical and ethical issues. It is also worth noting the way in which the students themselves may influence the secondary RE curriculum. Certainly, being a teenager involves existing in a space of questioning and exploration to which a philosophy and ethics approach is perhaps better suited. Having said this, in the experience of many secondary practitioners, this approach has tended to become a reductive exchange of under-developed opinions, rather than a robust engagement with philosophical theories (Ofsted 2013).

This is to do a disservice to the richness of the material available in Religious Education. It is not simply the case that younger pupils should focus on religious beliefs and teachings and older ones should explore philosophical and ethical questions. In the best classrooms, we see elements of each adapted to age-appropriate levels. We also see an approach to teaching that draws attention to internal diversity in belief systems and practice.

And yet, something is still missing. It seems odd to be teaching a subject about religions and beliefs without referencing the vast contribution made to these areas by theology. 'Theology' is a word that carries a weight of ambiguity and complexity. To some, it is a negative term, indicating dogmatism and oppressive authority (Brine 2016). To others, it indicates the intellectual discipline that grapples with questions about God, faith, life and death (Moulin 2015). In some areas of the world, theology is delivered through a particular lens of faith; in others, including the UK, theology can be a multidisciplinary academic approach to the study of religions and beliefs that requires neither faith nor belief (QAA 2014). From either standpoint, theology is an essential element in understanding religious belief and practice. It should take its place in the RE curriculum, in balance with philosophy and human sciences.

Redressing the balance

This proposal, part of a continuing dialogue, is still being shaped at the time of writing; the resulting framework is still in embryonic form. We advocate an approach to classroom practice that ensures a balance between the three disciplines of theology, philosophy and the social sciences. We believe it is crucial that children and young people investigate the subject matter of RE through the lenses of these disciplines, in order to gain deeper understanding and a more critical awareness of religion and belief. The future and sustainability of RE depends upon its ability to provide a balanced framework for the subject.

Theology

We are currently working with a definition of theology as – Conversations about foundational beliefs within religions and worldviews: examining the key ideas or concepts in religions and belief systems. The word 'theology' can mean 'study of God', although the richness of 'logos' implies knowledge, understanding and wisdom. It is inevitable that the study of religions and beliefs will include some approach to the concept of 'God' or 'Ultimate Reality'. However, religions and beliefs are not limited to these concepts. Looking through the lens of theology, as adapted from the work of Alister McGrath (2007), would enable pupils to consider:

- The origins of key ideas in a tradition; the sources of ideas, such as sacred texts, tradition, reason and experience; the reliability and authority of sources may also be debated.

- The ways in which the ideas have developed over time; how key ideas have changed through history, or have emerged at different points in response to societal events.

- The ways in which the ideas relate to one other; connections between different ideas, concepts and beliefs both within and between religions and beliefs.

- The ways in which theological ideas have been applied in the daily lives of believers; how theology impacts on the way believers see the world and, as a result, how they live their lives.

Theology involves investigating key texts and traditions within different religions and belief systems, exploring the ways in which they have been used as authoritative for believers, and the ways in which they have been challenged, interpreted and disregarded over time. It considers the use of reason in assessing the key ideas of a religion or belief system (thus crossing over with philosophy in places), as well as exploring the significance of experience on the claims made by religious and non-religious people. Theology enables children and young people to grapple with questions that have been raised by religions and beliefs over the centuries. Thus, we argue that everyone can have something to say about these ideas and concepts and that all can be theologians (QAA 2014).

Philosophy

We are currently working with a definition of philosophy as – Conversations about thinking: investigating the nature of knowledge, reality and morality, and the way in which we reason about them.

For many thousands of years, human beings have asked questions about meaning and existence. Around the sixth century BCE these questions began to be systematised in religious philosophies in different areas of the world. This is the starting point for the discipline of philosophy. However, curiosity on its own is not enough; people also have the capacity to reason as well as wonder. It is this process of reasoning that lies at the heart of philosophy. Philosophy is less about coming up with answers to difficult questions and more about the process of how people and communities try to answer them. It uses dialogue, discussion and debate to refine the way in which people think about the world and their place in it.

Philosophy contains three fields of enquiry that would be applicable to a balanced framework for RE. Looking through the lens of philosophy would enable pupils to consider:

- *Metaphysics*: the process of reasoning about existence and reality, and what might be beyond it; asking epistemological questions about how people know; what the object of study might reveal about the nature of existence and reality.

- *Logic*: investigating the process of reasoning that takes place when people ask questions about the world and their place in it; this branch of philosophy considers the way in which statements are put together to form conclusions, and whether they are asking reasonable questions of the object of study; as well as thinking about whether the object of study is providing a well-constructed and coherent response to questions such as existence, reality, truth or morality.

- *Moral philosophy*: considering the question 'What is a "good" life?', that is, what the object of study is telling believers about how to live a 'good' life.

Human and social sciences

We are currently working with a definition of human/social sciences as – Conversations about the human dimension of religions and beliefs: enquiring into the lived and diverse reality of religions and beliefs.

Religions and beliefs are not static entities that can be objectively studied. They are living and diverse, complex, sometimes chaotic, sometimes creative and always human

(Dinham and Shaw 2015; Jackson, Barratt and Everington 1994). This means that a balanced framework for RE needs to be mindful of not just what a religion or belief system says it is (the 'authoritative' version, as it were), but also the multiple ways in which it is lived. It is the difference between studying 'Christianity' and 'Christians', or 'Islam' and 'Muslims'. It is for this reason that the other two fields of enquiry are crucial, because the lived realities of religions and beliefs are often rooted in theological and philosophical interpretation. To that end, we have the opportunity to explore subject matter through the lens of social/human sciences. These disciplines include three fields of enquiry that would offer a valuable contribution to a balanced framework for RE. Looking through the lens of social sciences would enable pupils to consider:

- *Individual identities*: various human/social scientific disciplines (e.g. psychology, anthropology and sociology) consider questions of individual identity; how the object of study contributes to or impacts the individual identities of a believer.

- *Communal identities*: various human/social scientific disciplines (e.g. politics, anthropology and sociology) consider questions of communal identity; how the object of study contributes to or impacts communal identities within and beyond religions and belief systems.

- *Social structures*: various human/social scientific disciplines (e.g. politics, economics and sociology) consider questions about human society; how the object of study contributes to or impacts upon human patterns of life.

Engaging with the methodologies of the human and social sciences will help students investigate the ways in which religions, beliefs and religious believers have shaped and continue to shape societies around the world. They can promote better understanding of the ways in which religions and beliefs influence people's understanding of power, gender and compassion, among others. The methodology includes listening to the voices and observing the practice of members of faith and belief communities. Considering both the strengths and weaknesses of religions and beliefs in their lived reality is a crucial element of helping pupils hold the balanced and informed conversations we hope for.

Rebalancing issues

We have taken a pragmatic approach to the problem, and this means that we have not yet developed a theoretical framework for our proposal. We recognise the need to reflect further on issues around content and process: the three disciplines could be presented either as content to be studied, or as methodological processes to be followed, or a combination of both. It is for this reason that we have framed theology, philosophy and the human/social sciences as disciplines for the purposes of this manifesto. We recognise that these disciplines are both distinct and interrelated, so there will be a degree of crossover. The subject matter of theology, philosophy and the human/social sciences may well be appropriate for study at some levels more than others. In addition, we are aware that there may be other disciplines or approaches to knowledge we have not yet considered fully as part of our manifesto for balance.

A vision of rebalancing

We are going to illustrate our vision for the future of RE with two examples based on the different kinds of subject matter. We have both tried this out with teachers in recent months in order to help them think more deeply about the way they deliver and explore subject matter. These sessions have been based upon stimulus materials, such as images of festivals being celebrated, rituals taking place or artwork aimed at illustrating theological concepts such as creation.

As we are writing this chapter the festival of Diwali is being celebrated, so we decided to begin with this. We chose some pictures of Diwali being celebrated in Leicester that were available online, and decided to have a Key Stage I pupil in mind.

The theological lens offers questions such as 'How does this festival tell us something about good overcoming evil and why are these ideas important to Hindus?', 'Why is light an important symbol in this festival and what key belief does it symbolise?', 'How do Hindus use the symbol of light during the festival of Diwali and what does this tell us about the ways in which they live out important beliefs in day-to-day living?' These questions allow the children to enquire into the origins of Diwali and the concepts that underpin it, such as good versus evil and new beginnings. They also introduce the idea of different interpretations and responses to the meaning of Diwali, which may have an impact on how people celebrate the festival. In addition to this, they help pupils make connections between these concepts and the ways in which Hindus apply them in daily living. By enabling a more theological exploration of Diwali, standards in RE are raised.

We might then ask questions that look through the social/human scientific lens. For example, we might ask about what is happening in the stimulus material. How are people celebrating? Is it just Hindus who are celebrating? Some images do not show the traditional diva lamps that are often made in KSI classes, but rather huge decorations in the streets with parades, fireworks and dancing. People of all different ethnic and religious backgrounds might be taking part, many in what we might call Western clothing, not traditional Asian dress. This might help pupils ask questions about how participation in this celebration helps to contribute to individual and communal identities, both religious and social. Children might contrast this with Diwali celebrations in another city such as Mumbai. Or they might investigate the way another religious group such as the Jains or Sikhs celebrate the festival. This might help them better understand the ways in which religious affiliation impacts upon wider social structures and identities. Pupils might also analyse the stimulus material and weigh up how this celebration brings people together both within a religious community, as well as across religious and non-religious communities. These social/human scientific aspects of learning will help children to understand the lived reality of Diwali celebrations and the ways in which they contribute to individual, communal and social identities.

Lastly, the children might look through a more philosophical lens and consider the ways in which Diwali connects with a Hindu understanding of how to live a 'good life' (moral philosophy). This might be extended to explore other examples of ways in which issues of good and evil are expressed in the Hindu tradition. Pupils could analyse the way in which Sita and Ram make decisions in order to make a judgement about how their choices lead to the conclusion of the story. For example, Ram sees it as his duty to rescue Sita; pupils might therefore explore the way in which an understanding of 'duty' (*dharma*) impacts on the choices he makes. In addition to this, listening to and engaging with the Diwali narratives allows the children to understand how Hindus reason about and morally interpret the world around them.

Inquiring into Diwali through the lenses of these three disciplines provides a broad and balanced approach which is challenging and engaging, and reflects the complex lived reality of religion in the world today. It enables children to gain knowledge of this dharmic tradition by exploring not only key concepts, such as dharma, karma and moksha, but also the diverse practices and bhakti associated with Diwali. It provides opportunities for children to analyse beliefs and traditions within Hinduism, particularly those contained in the Ramayana, whilst also offering space for their own responses to the knowledge and understanding they encounter.

Our second example considers the way in which a KS3 student might engage with a different form of religious observance that takes place around the same time as Diwali. All Saints Day and

All Souls Day are marked by various Christian denominations on the 1st and 2nd of November respectively. The former is about remembering the saints of the Church, and the latter is about praying for the souls of the departed. The Mexican Day of the Dead celebrations, a syncretistic festival that incorporates both Christian and indigenous polytheistic traditions, usually take place between 31st October and 2nd November.

A KS3 approach to studying these events could start with a metaphysical investigation into the ways in which human beings define life and death and, crucially, the transition between the two. Viewing this topic through a philosophical lens, students may further extend their understanding through an investigation of the ethical issues related to our understanding of life and death, such as those relating to end-of-life care and the concept of an afterlife. This will help them consider the ways in which these observances relate to religious beliefs about right and wrong and what constitutes a 'good' life. Students might also enquire into sources relating to near-death experiences, using the tools of metaphysics to draw conclusions about the validity – or not – of such experiences. At this higher level of learning, they might also be given the opportunity to study a range of philosophical treatises (e.g. Epicurus's *Letter to Menoeceus*, Plato's *Phaedo* or Boethius's *Consolations of Philosophy*) focusing on analysing the process of reasoning that is taking place.

Further study of these religious observances would lead naturally into considering theological questions such as 'What do Christians mean by the soul?', 'What do different Christian denominations believe about life after death?' and 'How is sainthood defined in different Christian traditions?' These questions allow students to consider the origins of the key concepts and ideas that lie at the heart of the celebrations. Students could explore the varying interpretations of Christian doctrines that are underpinned by the celebrations, including sainthood, eternal life, heaven, hell and purgatory. They may look at the ways in which these key concepts and ideas have changed over time within and between Christian denominations.

Understanding the key concepts and the various ways in which they are interpreted will help students understand the diversity of practices associated with the festival, such as the offering of a Requiem Mass for the dead.

The way in which students enquire into these celebrations should not only be focused on these philosophical and theological interpretations; they must also reflect the impact of cultural and sociological factors. All Souls and All Saints Days in the UK and the Day of the Dead in Mexico have all been influenced by pre-Christian belief systems. In the UK, the date of the celebrations is linked with other festivals. It may, for example, be connected to a Celtic festival of the dead that was celebrated on 1st November. Celebrations are also influenced by popular culture. The students might ask what impact popular culture has on traditional religious observances and the ways in which they contribute to individual, communal and social identities. They might compare the way other festivals and celebrations have changed over time and led to increased diversity of practice. They might discuss whether it is the family that is at the heart of such commemorations, as many Mexicans would argue, rather than big parades and festivities as evidenced by the 2016 Day of the Dead celebrations in Mexico City (see Agrin 2016). This would help students analyse the ways in which religious observances impact on communities and social structures, and vice versa, thus giving them a more rounded and balanced understanding of the religions and beliefs being studied. It is by investigating these religious observances through all three lenses that students will gain a deep, balanced and well-informed understanding.

The value of rebalancing

Balance is often missing from current practice in RE. This is not to deny that many pupils are accessing high-quality and deep learning in RE. We have taken a pragmatic approach to a particular problem we have observed as advisers. As a consequence, we feel it would be possible to provide a nationally recognised curriculum framework that would enable any subject matter covered in the classroom to be delivered in a balanced way. We acknowledge that the boundaries between the three disciplines are fluid: they are interdependent, constantly in conversation with each other, and sometimes in competition. Nevertheless, they have value as a means of structuring an RE framework fit for the 21st century. This approach could potentially bring together different epistemological views and unite a diverse RE community. As educators, our priority must be to provide a framework that is practical, challenging and, above all, balanced.

Acknowledgements

We are indebted to Jane Chipperton and Olivia Seymour for engaging in this dialogue along with us over the last two years and playing a significant role in shaping this proposal (Chipperton *et al.* 2016). We would like to express our thanks to the many colleagues who have critiqued, challenged and supported our proposals in our endeavour to ensure balanced Religious Education for all.

References

Agrin, D. (2016, 30 October) 'Mexico City's James Bond-inspired Day of the Dead parade gets mixed reviews'. *The Guardian*. Accessed 27 May 2017 at www.theguardian.com/world/2016/oct/29/day-of-the-dead-parade-james-bond-mexico-city

Brine, A. (2016, 3 May) 'Thinking theologically in RE? Part 2' [Blog post]. RE:Online. Accessed 27 May 2017 at www.reonline.org.uk/news/alans-blog-thinking-theologically-in-re-part-2-alan-brine

Chipperton, J., Georgiou, G., Seymour, O. and Wright, K. (2016, 5 July) 'Revision: Rethinking RE – a conversation about religious and theological literacy.' RE:Online. Accessed 27 May 2017 at www.reonline.org.uk/news/revision-rethinking-re-a-conversation-about-religious-and-theological-literacy

Church of England (2014) *Making a Difference? A Review of Religious Education in Church of England Schools*. London: Church House.

Dinham, A. and Shaw, M. (2015) *RE for Real: The Future of Teaching and Learning About Religion and Belief.* London: Goldsmiths University.

Jackson, R. (1997) *Religious Education: An Interpretive Approach.* London: Hodder and Stoughton.

Jackson, R., Barratt, M. and Everington, J. (1994) *Bridges to Religions: Teacher's Resource Book.* Oxford: Heinemann.

McGrath, A. (2007) *Christian Theology: An Introduction* (4th edn). Oxford: Blackwell Publishing.

Moulin, D. (2015) 'We need theological religious education, not politicised religious education.' RE:Online. Accessed 27 May 2017 at www.reonline. org.uk/news/think-piece-we-need-theological-religious-education-not-politicised-religious-education-daniel-moulin

Ofsted (2013) *Religious Education: Realising the Potential.* Accessed on 25 May 2017 at www.gov.uk/government/publications/religious-education-realising-the-potential

QAA (2014) *Subject Benchmark: Statement Theology and Religious Studies.* Accessed 27 May 2017 at www.qaa.ac.uk/en/Publications/Documents/SBS-theology-religious-studies.pdf

Chapter 7

TOWARDS A CORE INTEGRITY FOR RELIGIOUS EDUCATION

SUSHMA SAHAJPAL

RE faces a number of contemporary challenges: these include children's rights to cultural identity and wellbeing, the historical and current contradictions in the pedagogy of RE, and the marginalisation and belittling of spiritual, moral, social and cultural dimensions of education as a whole. To face these challenges successfully, RE needs to transform itself. In a contemporary multi-faith school community, set in a complex connected global context, the need for RE is critical, but the subject needs to be updated. This chapter argues that RE can be revived through a new focus on meaning, value and purpose. This new model could help to nurture children's identity through an 'insider' human perspective that critically and creatively explores what it means to be human, using a number of perspectives and accessing knowledge in a number of religious or philosophical systems. Referencing the UN Convention on the Rights of the Child, and a range of educational philosophers, this manifesto calls for a core integrity of RE, and describes what it might ask of teachers.

Integrity and identity: Placing the child's human rights at the core of RE

The UN Convention on the Rights of the Child 1989 is a useful measure for evaluating the current purpose and aims of RE, and evolving these to a new set of aims that prioritise both the needs of the child and our aspirations as a society. The rights enshrined in the Convention cover many aspects beyond the scope of RE. However, they frequently move between cultural, linguistic, religious and personal identities, mentioning wellbeing, freedom and discrimination, and specifying some ways in which adults and organisations are expected to respect the rights of the child. It is these rights that we need to consider in revisioning a fit-for-purpose RE.

Article 2 of the Convention sets out a foundational principle that children's rights are to be respected 'without discrimination of any kind', and that measures should be taken to 'ensure that the child is protected against all forms of discrimination'. The full weight of this is felt later when we read that Article 12 identifies the child's right to be heard, 13 protects the child's freedom of expression and 14 calls for respect for the child's freedom of thought, conscience and religion. Article 30 extends rights of enjoyment of their own culture to the children of ethnic, religious or linguistic minorities, including the right to practise and profess their own religion and speak their own language.

Article 3 calls for primary consideration to be given to the best interests of the child: children's wellbeing should be enshrined by 'all appropriate legislative and administrative measures'. This is echoed later on in care for their physical and mental health (Article 25), and in a call for education systems to be directed to 'development of the child's personality, talents and mental and physical abilities', and 'preparation of the child for responsible life in a free society' (Article 29).

The specific rights mentioned above create responsibilities for individual adults, for the small-scale societies that schools are, and for the administrative and legal machinery that governs schools and subjects. These rights, when considered alongside RE, expose aspects of our subject that have untapped potential. If RE wants to use this potential, it must repurpose and refocus itself as a curriculum subject. It must audit and adapt its current dominant pedagogical models, move on from polarising debates and find its integrity in serving the educational needs of the child.

At the heart of education: The potential in the curriculum

The educational needs of the child in Britain were revisited in 2010, when the English National Curriculum was reviewed. One of the leading intellectual influencers was Tim Oates, who chaired the review panel and articulated criticisms of previous models of the curriculum. Oates called for curriculum design to have coherence, by which he meant that aims, content, pedagogy and assessment would all be aligned with each other to produce high-quality teaching and learning. He noted the lack of coherence in previous curriculum models as a significant contributor to poor performance in England when compared to other education systems (Oates 2010). He later identified several 'public goods' that education could offer, including 'discipline-specific knowledge, skills and understanding in [a] broad range of disciplines, orientation to learning, learning to learn, physical and mental well-being, and personal and social identity' (Oates 2012, p.3).

Oates, no particular advocate for the rights of the child or for a spiritual vision for education, nevertheless can be called in evidence for the confused and contested nature of curriculum provision, and its lack of clarity about purpose. His call for curriculum coherence and identification of education's public goods imply that there can and should be an integrated human and social purpose across all subjects, a vision that has been shared by many others. Such a vision is often spoken of using the language of spiritual, moral, social and cultural development, usually shortened to SMSC.

The centrality of SMSC is in principle a long-standing feature of maintained schools in England. The current curriculum framework requires schools to provide a curriculum that, among other priorities, 'promotes the spiritual, moral, cultural, mental, and physical development of pupils at the school, and of society' (Department for Education 2014b, p.1). This aspiration has existed since 1944. However, in the current version of the curriculum it is hard to see how the curriculum's writers envisage SMSC being translated into everyday curriculum provision. It does not appear in the overall curriculum aims. The government's most recent non-statutory guidance on SMSC connects it to the four fundamental British values. It mentions an approach across the whole curriculum, and encourages schools in making sure that pupils have a voice that is listened to; but it does not mention any subjects by name, and gives no guidance on how these aspects might be embedded (Department for Education 2014a).

One notable exception is the purpose statement in the programme of study for English, which recognises the subject's importance in broad human terms that touch briefly on spirituality and human rights:

> Through reading in particular, pupils have a chance to develop culturally, emotionally, intellectually, socially and spiritually... pupils who do not learn to speak, read and write fluently and confidently are effectively disenfranchised. (Department for Education 2013, p.1)

While it is good to see this recognition given to the human rights and spiritual and cultural dimensions of education, I would like to extend this interpretation to a core competency to be developed through every subject. I envisage these aspects not as occasional, optional 'add-ons', but as hallmarks of an educated person, as crucial as literacy and numeracy. Yet with no measurable SMSC outcomes specified, or curriculum subject allocated to lead on this, this aspiration seems unlikely to be fulfilled.

A vision lost and found

Such an aspiration is not new: it features in the liberal tradition of education, for example in Alfred North Whitehead's call to teachers to reject 'scraps of information' and 'inert ideas' in favour of a higher vision of cultural sensibility, facility with using and applying ideas, and appreciation of the present (Whitehead 1929, p.1). His claim for 'the essence of education' (p.14) is a distillation of his belief, shared by many others then and now, that teaching and learning are to be understood as sacred activities. More recently, the passionate protest that education has descended into dominant utilitarian and economic aims, losing its vision of human development and personal meaning, has been voiced by many (e.g. Postman 1995; Pring 2004). Richard Pring in particular gives voice to those in subject communities – in this case, History, but the argument could be applied to any subject – that teachers can and should initiate their pupils lovingly into their subject discipline (Pring 2013). Equally important, the objection that schooling is too often a denial and destruction of children's creativity (Robinson 2006) finds wide resonance among teachers. The argument that children have a right to be recognised by several, multiple definitions of intelligence, not just one (Gardner 1984), has also taken root. Gardner's way of describing personal intelligences, based on psychological observation, tracks the growing child's sense of a self that is deeply layered and culturally responsive. Gardner believes that this sense of self is and must be teachable, in other words that instruction and discovery of wisdom in this personal realm is both possible and necessary, 'an ineluctable aspect of the human condition and one firmly rooted in our species membership' (p.255).

In the current curriculum, we see traces of SMSC given a tokenistic and fragmented place at the margins, with economic and utilitarian models afforded pride of place. In recent decades the teaching profession has been pressured to systematise its work in a mistaken view that this was professionalising it. We see the UN vision of the child's right to a cultural identity and a voice given a similarly small portion, with more energy going to information-based models of received knowledge. Many educationalists with a higher vision, living and departed, are part of what we might call a transcendent tradition: both in the sense that they emphasise the sacredness of learning, and also in the sense that they go far beyond the present limited aims. These are voices we need to hear again today. Children as young humans are engaged in a developmental process that should not be ours to mechanise, only to cultivate and resource as best we can. In the pressure to achieve accountability measures, the deeper educational needs of the child are being neglected and need to be re-championed. RE may be uniquely equipped to lead on these if it is willing to engage with the challenge.

Building on the transcendent tradition: Three human-centred focuses for education

I wish to amplify the voices that have called for a more human and humane vision of education, for teachers at large and for RE in particular. With Whitehead on the curriculum, I would wish to argue that while knowledge is valuable, its acquisition is only a crucial stepping-stone in a process of becoming, which includes but ultimately supersedes knowledge. With Pring, I would wish to reinstate the human, scholarly and moral purposes of education, the love of subject and the understanding and care for pupils. With Robinson, I would celebrate creativity and imagination as central to being a child and a learner. With Gardner, I would underline the importance of the whole person as intelligent and gifted in many ways, and as the true subject of education. With Oates, I would reinstate the public goods of education, particularly those concerned with the love of learning, and with him I would call for this to be coherently aligned across the aims and content of the whole curriculum, as well as assessment. I would make a distinction between being educated as a way of being, and being qualified as a demonstrable measure of performance and competency.

This speaks to an inclusive society where, though everyone may not achieve qualification, everyone can be educated.

If the education system succeeds in embedding knowledge acquisition within a broader, deeper purpose for the child, this helps to shift the identity of any subject, and particularly RE. For our subject, the focus could shift from choices about which sects of which religions to study, to prioritising what children need to know and understand about human community and identity, and its diverse responses to the 'big questions' of life: life's meaning, value and purpose.

Such a broader deeper purpose for education could be based on three human focuses deduced from Tim Oates' 'public goods of education'. These three, in full support of the UN Convention's rights of the child, are strong personal identity, wellbeing and a learning disposition. These three focuses could empower RE with a simpler, more successful educational identity; they could unleash more of its potential, and help to contribute to the legal aspiration of SMSC not only in schools but also in wider society.

In prioritising pupils' strong personal identity and associated empathic skills, RE shifts away from insider/outsider binaries and allows pupils confidently to connect to the humanity of others of their own or another tradition without undermining their own or others' beliefs. I believe this approach, where children develop as the 'experts' in their own experience, expert witnesses of others' experiences, as well as students of worldly knowledge, is crucial in RE. The field of study is all that is most sacred to humanity, including to the students themselves.

In focusing on pupils' wellbeing, RE could move beyond subjective/objective binaries to adopt a position in which wellbeing is promoted through self-knowledge and mutually respectful testimonial exploration and classroom dialogue as part of a wider cultural milieu.

In focusing on developing a learning disposition, RE can think of pupils and teachers as partners in discovery. Such a disposition would include engagement with big questions; curiosity about religious, philosophical and cultural identity as mediated through language and symbols; sensibility in using their own and others' language and symbols; and the ability to encounter an unknown other with both compassion and what I would like to call 'an educated curiosity'.

The teacher's own disposition is also relevant. I like Hannam's description of the RE teacher's agency in his/her disposition. Even though the teacher is an authority figure, 'a representative of the existing order of things' (Hannam 2016, p.116), to be effective he/she must change and develop in ways that go beyond reason, intellect or normal professional development. He/she must also be 'open to change to discovering new ways of existing in the world' (p.116), suggesting that the classroom exploration of the field of study can be an exciting frontier of knowledge. Here students and teachers may learn from each other, particularly where a student's own religious identity can extend the class's knowledge.

The learning disposition is particularly fertile for RE: the subject of study is itself evolving as traditions, communities and individuals continue to adapt faster than textbooks and resources can keep pace with. A teacher can only facilitate encounter with sufficient knowledge of the world as it is currently perceived. The world includes their own identity within it, along with skills, knowledge and learning dispositions. Congruently, many RE teachers are already doing this, in creating the oft-named 'safe space' of RE. This is something that RE teachers should not and need not be pressurised to surrender in a stampede to be like other subjects. I also believe this is a way in which other subjects can be empowered to learn from and extend themselves to be more like RE. In an integrated curriculum they could embrace the potency that SMSC and these three human focuses may bring to their respective subjects and students' learning journeys.

Meaning, value and purpose (MVP):
A new positioning for RE

Thus in a new RE-integrated curriculum, where each subject is embedded with its full quota of SMSC as well as academic learning, RE could take an evolutionary step to be both academically rigorous and humanely sensitive in how it deals with the religious and cultural identities of the children in, and not in, the room. It can model how to interact with each other as confident individuals in a multi-faith space. This would be a transition from an intention to understand what it means to be part of the Christian (or any other) faith – a normative enquiry in current RE – to a new purpose, aiming to understand what it means to be part of the human race from multiple perspectives. This enquiry would aim to discover how any community being studied derives meaning (M), ascribes value (V) and seeks purpose (P). MVP is a sacred quest for individuals and communities. The knowledge field for MVP would be those human communities that engage in the quest and live meaningful, value-informed, purposeful lives. The communities might be Abrahamic, Dharmic, Pagan or non-religious. Part of the critical enquiry in MVP is to examine the accuracy of our models: the criticality is not directed at practitioners' faith claims (not appropriate in a school) but at how well as scholars we have understood our evidence of an MVP community. For example, we would be always asking ourselves, and the pupils, to evaluate our understanding of sacred texts, visiting speakers, art, architecture or other forms of expression. There would be a continuing critique and refinement of our own modelling methods and enquiry approaches. This would be a foundation for being able to approach and engage confidently and constructively with a range of people and places with different MVP identities.

A liberated, self-determined RE could focus on high-quality, academically challenging, discipline-specific knowledge skills and understanding. Other subjects, fulfilling their role in SMSC, could learn much from this model. I suggest that RE has as much to distribute of its attributes to other subjects, as it has to receive from them. One of the ways of doing this would be to identify measurable, publishable attributes of SMSC and specify them as part of the purpose of RE, as in reality it is what will be measured that is valued most in today's resource-stretched schools. This would underscore what I believe could be RE's true status in the future, as a leading curriculum subject, delivering a core competency, and whose true siblings are the core subjects at the heart of the curriculum, rather than the humanities.

RE, in its present condition, continues to wrestle with a number of binary problems. I am concerned about the insider/outsider dissonance and confusion that currently sits in the unresolved heart of RE. Once we accept that we cannot assume objectivity, it becomes important to embrace the multiple ways that all humans carry shades of insider and outsider. This speaks to the importance of a non-partisan approach that could work with an MVP model where some learning is likely to be similar to the student's identity, and some different. MVP is not a way of classifying or differentiating between faiths; rather it opens the door to seeing overlaps between them, as well as studying multi-faith and new communities. It is an intention-driven inclusive lens for accessing and inspecting any actual human community.

For any MVP community being taught, the teacher's intention must be to teach as if a child of that age-group from that faith tradition is in the room, along with another child who knows nothing about it. This incorporates the 'learning about us' and 'learning about them' as a dynamic warp and weft of studying aspects of human meaning-making in a pluralist way. Humanity is inherently pluralist, but humans are instinctively singularist. Education must tackle this. The teacher's intention must be to reassure learners that in the classroom we have dynamic membership of multiple groups: that 'some of us' is sometimes you, sometimes not you. Content coverage must be determined by students in the room, so they all experience some 'us' and some 'them'.

Pupils can also learn to interpret consciously and skilfully, to be able to switch lenses with deliberation, to engage with alternative and multiple perspectives, and to become skilled in choosing when and how to be critical, compassionate, empathic or academic in their encounters. To develop such skills, a diversity of encounters is required.

MVP offers a rationale from which to engage with commonality and diversity within and between communities, and interrogate and positively adjust existing pedagogies as well as craft new ones. As purpose and outcomes are thus brought into alignment, we can have a coherent, consistent integrity to the subject in all schools nationally. My hope is that schools with a religious character could engage in this with their own material.

Some case studies and further work beyond this manifesto would be required to illustrate how pupils would make progress and be assessed with integrity. Part of a core humanity competency is increasing agility in moving fluently between a number of perspectives. For example, progress could be evidenced by confidently participating in discussions of aspects of one's own faith tradition (e.g. Hindu), like me (e.g. performing Hindu Puja) and not like me (e.g. eating fish), or someone of a 'different faith' (e.g. a Muslim), who is like me (e.g. a sari-wearing Bangladeshi) and not like me (e.g. worshipping in a mosque).

Conclusion

Human potential is not individual: it is identified, nurtured, realised and fulfilled in community and connection with other human beings. Ultimately MVP is about studying ways of modelling and understanding 'us', to take up our places, rights and identities as part of a free society. It invites pupils and teachers to see themselves as part of an evolving species, collaboratively developing a changing knowledge-set from multiple perspectives. Each adult generation is called to bring the finest, most educated aspects of itself to the attention of children while teaching them discernment, literacy and a measurable SMSC, so that what emerges from them moves us all forward.

This core integrity can be an excitingly agile model for RE, robust enough to serve children in diverse school communities, and responsive enough to evolve as belief patterns evolve. An educationally valid, research-based rationale can provide profession-level signposting leading us out of conundrums on depth and breadth of coverage of faith-traditions. Such a rationale would have the advantage of enabling curriculum designers to navigate their way appropriately and transparently through a vast field of knowledge, and wider society to support resources being allocated to a transparently beneficial endeavour. Far from being a burden for schools, this new core integrity for RE has the potential to be education's MVP in another sense: its most valued player.

References

Department for Education (2013) *National Curriculum for England: English Programme of Study*. London: DfE.

Department for Education (2014a) *Promoting Fundamental British Values as Part of SMSC in Schools: Departmental Advice for Maintained Schools*. London: DfE.

Department for Education (2014b) *Statutory Guidance: National Curriculum in England: Framework for Key Stages 1 to 4*. London: DfE.

Gardner, H. (1984) *Frames of Mind: The Theory of Multiple Intelligences*. London: William Heinemann.

Hannam, P. (2016) *What Should Religious Education Aim to Achieve? An Investigation into the Purpose of Religious Education in the Public Sphere*. Unpublished PhD thesis, Stirling University.

Oates, T. (2010) *Could Do Better: Using International Comparisons to Refine the National Curriculum in England*. Cambridge: Cambridge Assessment.

Oates, T. (2012) *Control and Autonomy: A Key Issue in Debates on School Curricula and National Curriculum*. Cambridge: Cambridge Assessment.

Postman, N. (1995) *The End of Education*. New York, NY: Vintage Books.

Pring, R. (2004) *Philosophy of Education*. London and New York, NY: Continuum.

Pring, R. (2013) 'Why teach history, anyway?' Unpublished address to the Annual Conference of History Teachers Network, Institute of Education, London.

Robinson, K. (2006) 'Do Schools Kill Creativity?' TED Talk. Accessed 27 May 2017 at www.ted.com/talks/ken_robinson_says_schools_kill_creativity www.sirkenrobinson.com

Whitehead, A. (1929) *The Aims of Education*. New York, NY: Free Press.

Part 2

FUTURES

INTRODUCTION

John Dewey (1859–1952) believed that teaching is a sophisticated and complex activity and that teachers need not only to know what they plan to teach but also to be sure and articulate in their reasons for teaching it. Dewey called this underpinning vision and philosophy of education an art that the artist/teacher needs to draw out from within themselves.

> It is difficult always to be a creative artist. I think, however, that we should get on more rapidly if we realise that, if education is going to live up to its profession, it must be seen as a work of art which requires the same qualities of personal enthusiasm and imagination as are required by the musician, painter or artist. Each of these artists needs a technique which is more or less mechanical, but in the degree to which he loses his personal vision to become subordinate to the more formal rules of the technique he falls below the level and grade of the artist. He becomes reduced again to the level of the artisan who follows the blue prints, drawings, and plans that are made by others. (Dewey 2008, p.186)

The authors and chapters in the second part of this book present clear philosophies of education: of planning, teaching and learning. Their contexts are clearly set within the Religious Education classroom and their focuses are the pupils and their teachers. This part is called 'Futures' because the lessons to be gleaned from these chapters offer food for thought to nourish deep learning in Religious Education. The authors grapple with challenging issues that face the subject, and share ways in which they are addressing the challenges. No one can teach another how to be an artist. As Dewey explains, the learning of skills and techniques makes for a proficient artisan, but the artist arises from effective technique inspired by a clear vision and aspiration. These chapters do not hold remedies to the challenges facing RE; rather, they offer accounts of thinking, planning, teaching and learning that will, hopefully, prompt further thinking, planning, teaching and learning in RE lessons to the benefit of pupils, teachers and a wider society.

Three chapters (Mary Myatt, Mike Castelli, Phil Champain) offer ways of planning and teaching, pedagogies, that set pupils' learning within specific rather than general contexts. The specific context offers encounters with individuals, their beliefs and practices, in a manner that moves away from the abstract and generic study of a religion or worldview to a dialogue with individuals and communities that helps pupils frame specific, open questions, which they can pose in a manner that not only asks questions of others but also pushes the question back on the interrogator and their beliefs and practices. Learning how to frame key questions for self and another are major steps in learning. Two of the authors (Neil McKain, Adam Whitlock) share their refusal to dodge some of the most challenging political and social issues facing RE locally, nationally and globally. Their accounts of their responses to these challenges illustrate positive futures that benefit their pupils, their schools and the status of the subject. The role of faith communities in shaping contemporary RE is often contentious, and Derek Holloway does not shy away from this in his chapter. His account of the history of the Anglican community's role in English RE under the designation of 'generous hospitality' makes a positive case for the Anglican community's involvement that may be a model for other faith communities. Dawn Cox presents a contentious analysis of the interface between academic research and classroom practice and proposes some positive ways forward for RE that would not only benefit classroom practitioners but also enhance the relevance of academic research itself. James

Robson provides much convincing evidence and information on the role of online engagement as a key contemporary learning tool of teachers of RE and for the future. The chapter is also a challenge to those who are not already members of this growing community.

This part offers many challenges, but these are realistic and practical challenges for the subject and its teachers that not only illustrate why we need to talk about RE but also how doing so may offer positive futures for both.

Reference

Dewey, J. (2008) *The Middle Works of John Dewey, 1899–1924: Vol 15. Journal Articles, Essays, and Miscellany Published in the 1923–1924 Period* (J.A. Boydston, ed.) Carbondale, IL: Southern Illinois University Press.

Chapter 8

MAKING THE CASE FOR MORE DEMANDING RELIGIOUS EDUCATION

MARY MYATT

This chapter makes the case that too much RE is being dumbed down, and that this is not serving pupils' needs. Pupils themselves say that they appreciate opportunities to do difficult work that stretches them and makes them think.

Introduction

We are a challenge-seeking species. In our own time, whether children or adults, we enjoy doing things that stretch us and make us think. The range of crosswords, sudoku, maths and word puzzles are testament to the fact that companies are making millions of pounds' profit from the fact that we like 'testing' ourselves. We would not be doing this if things were easy. The point is that they are difficult, and we take cognitive pleasure from the fact that we persevere through the difficult conundrums to get to the end. The pleasure and satisfaction is from the concentration required to think a problem through and get to the right answer eventually. This would be denied if the process were too easy. The same might be said for the electronic versions of 'testing' ourselves, such as Minecraft, where the increase in difficulty is related to satisfaction at reaching a certain stage and then being enticed into the next level.

Motivation

The process here relies on intrinsic motivation. This is quite different from extrinsic motivation where the rewards are the approval of others, the achievement of grades and the satisfaction of achieving at a certain level. There is nothing wrong with extrinsic motivation, but intrinsic motivation is a stronger driver. It comes from a deep, personal satisfaction that hard work, which did not fall into place immediately, is deeply rewarding. And it is this which I believe is a neglected aspect of planning for learning that is evident across the curriculum in general and in Religious Education in particular. This is by no means an issue in every case, but I argue that the quality and quantity of what is offered to pupils could be made more demanding.

Deep engagement

The reason why planning for learning is not framed around appropriate difficulty is, I believe, a result of misguided notions about pupils' self-esteem. In many cases, the preservation of pupils' self-esteem is at the expense of deep learning. This manifests in classrooms where pupils are given low-level tasks, often based around worksheets, where one word or limited responses are sufficient, and where the teacher signs off low-quality answers as 'fantastic' or 'brilliant' when they are anything but. This is because there is a reluctance to expect pupils to explain their thinking, expose their misunderstanding and be expected to modify or deepen their answers. The swift signing-off also has to do with an urgent need to cover the curriculum content. However, this is at the expense of a deep engagement of the material that develops children's intellectual architecture both in terms of understanding key concepts and ideas, and of how these relate to the lived world of religion and their own development as thoughtful human beings.

The second reason why low-level work is expected of many pupils is a confusion between the 'learning about' and 'learning from' religion. In many cases the learning about has been small gobbet facts, offering no line of enquiry to a big idea or concept, after which pupils are expected to make some shallow comparisons about the worth of these, such as whether they like them or not. This way of planning for learning sells our pupils short.

So, our pupils are capable of more, should be encouraged to get to a place where they struggle, and they need to be supported to get there. This is what cognitive science has to offer to the argument: Dan Willingham (2009) argues that humans are curious, but thinking is hard; that learning is deepest when it is framed around problems to be solved; that pupils have an entitlement to conception knowledge that enables rich connections; that teachers provide opportunities to encounter the 'meaning' of the material and that this is best achieved through the power of stories, conflicts and dilemmas. Similarly, Peter Brown *et al.* (2014) argue that learning should be full of effort, and Doug Lemov (2012) makes the case for there being no opt-out, no half-answers; that these answers should be stretched by asking for reasoning and checking with other pupils; that pupils should answer in complete sentences using correct grammar; that there should be no cheap praise; and finally that mistakes are good as they are triggers for new learning.

Challenge

Challenge is perceived to be a good thing, but it is surrounded by confusion. The concept of challenge is now recognised as an important part of curriculum planning. However, it is not the following: it is not extension, it is not another 'thing' to do; it is not more of the same. It is, instead, the offering of demanding material, in which the key concepts and ideas can be explored from a very early age, which then provide a framework for talk, thought, misconceptions and deep engagement. Every child is entitled to this. And it is the obligation of every teacher to work out how to provide it.

The paradox is that in thinking about deep challenge as an entitlement for every child, there is actually less work for the teacher. While this is not the primary aim, rather the offering of a rich banquet for children, it nevertheless means less fiddly preparation of fancy resources and shallow marking for the teacher. This in itself can become a problem as we are used to being busy, to preparation of lots of 'stuff' and then 'marking' it. And it is important to step back from this and to ask: Is this really rich, difficult stuff for my pupils or is it busy stuff which is a substitute for deep learning? What is happening in many schools is that teachers are spending time researching and preparing resources, which are often tasks or things to do and which provide little opportunity to develop and demonstrate understanding. An example of this is a worksheet showing the inside of a synagogue. The pupils are expected to label this and to say a few words about it, often with prompts from a box at the bottom of the page. In this example, what pupils need to be able to do is extract information and link it to the artefacts within the building. But what they don't get is an understanding of the significance of these in the lives of Jewish people. This is not the fault of the teacher who believes that they are giving them information and has 'proof' from the collected worksheets (which are later stuck into books) that their pupils have learnt some key facts about the Jewish synagogue. What is missing is any planning for securing pupils' deep understanding of the importance of these. The task has masked understanding.

What is needed is fewer things done in greater depth. So, for instance, to take the example of a *mezuzah*, again from the Jewish tradition: in many classrooms, this is presented as box that contains passages from the Torah and acts as a reminder of the importance of living the obligations and expectations of the covenant via the *mitzvoth* on a daily basis. So, on a surface level, the pupils know a bit and they might have written a few words about it. What they have not got is any sense of the importance of the covenant and how this daily reminder links them back to the earliest Jewish traditions and obligations.

Task or understanding?

The example above is a case of confusing the task with understanding, with the completion of a worksheet as the work, rather than a richer, more complex offer that requires pupils to struggle, to think deeply and to produce work over time.

There is a very helpful analogy created by the Swiss Cottage School (2015) that illustrates the difference between classic planning and planning that has real purpose, allows for struggle and that has an authentic outcome. In the Swiss Cottage example, there are two pupils 'A' and 'B'. The learning intention is for the pupils to 'learn to play the guitar'. Teacher A gives Pupil A a list of things he needs to know – name the colour of the guitar, pluck the strings of the guitar, etc. Over time, Teacher A ticks off the list of things that Pupil A has achieved and proudly reports that he is working at a 'higher level'. When a visitor comes to the classroom to talk to Pupil A about what he has learnt and asks him a few questions, he is not able to answer. On the other hand, Teacher B sets the learning intention for Pupil B as 'to perform in front of a live audience'. Pupil B starts by learning a few chords alongside his teacher, making mistakes and practising, sometimes going backwards, sometimes making mistakes, sometimes getting frustrated. When the visitor arrives, he finds Pupil B performing his own composition in front of an audience.

The difference here is that one set of learning was framed in terms of tasks, while the other was framed in terms of an authentic 'product' at the end, in this case a performance. When we think about this in terms of the Religious Education example above, the difference in thinking about the final learning would have made all the difference. The worksheets would have been fine if they were eventually going to provide pupils with an opportunity to demonstrate the link between the artefacts and their importance for the Jewish community. What happened instead was that busy worksheets masked the paucity of learning. The metrics for measuring children's learning were limited to the completion of the task. So, what needed to happen to make this worthwhile, to include struggle and to make sure that pupils were properly challenged?

Well, for one thing, it is pointless trying to do the inside of a synagogue in one lesson. We need to resist the temptation to race through content, because this is usually at the expense of pupils' learning. What is needed instead is some thought about what these artefacts are really saying and symbolising. How do they fit into the history, tradition and practice for the Jewish community? How might a Jewish child encounter them and have them explained? What are the sources for these? In the case of the *mezuzah*, rather than doing a surface explanation with pupils filling in closed questions, showing a superficial understanding, the learning needs to be stretched in order to allow greater depth. In this case, either an actual artefact or a high-quality visual image would provide pupils with something to look at and talk about. It would provide an opportunity for speculation, for questions, for research – What is this? Where might we find it? What's inside it? Why is it in a Jewish home? This process would lead into the importance for Jewish families of remembering the *mitzvoth* as a way of daily connection to the covenant. It would provide an opportunity for pupils to read the inscription, find it in the Torah and speculate about why this is still relevant for Jewish families today; and it would provide an opportunity for pupils to create a 'product' that gives insight into their knowledge and understanding in a way that answering a few low-level questions on a worksheet could never do.

Products

A word about 'products' – these are referenced by Tim Oates (2014) in discussing the National Curriculum without levels. Products give us insight into what pupils know, understand and can do on their own terms – this might be what they write and their scores on tests, which might show the gaps in their knowledge, the artefacts they produce and the things that they say. In the case above, the product could be pupils' talk about the significance of the *mezuzah*; it might be a piece of extended writing that shows their thinking, their research and their findings. All this is significantly richer than the completion of a worksheet. The former provides the teacher with rich insights into pupils' learning and the extent to which they have mastered the subject, while the latter provides a poor substitute for learning. Most importantly there are opportunities for stretching pupils' thinking, for creating the conditions where there are no easy answers and for which there will be an element of struggle. It is this deeper layer of complexity that provides the challenge, rather than another 'thing' to do. It also creates the conditions for pupils to be able to demonstrate mastery of this aspect of their learning. There is some confusion about mastery – a pupil has mastered something if they are able to talk, write or do something on their own terms about something that they have learnt. The paradox of mastery is that it both takes learning to a deeper space, but also opens up new vistas, so mastery holds both depth and a realisation that there is still so much more to know and understand. Worksheets with narrow tasks in them do not provide this opportunity.

What pupils say

Turning to what pupils say about their learning, I draw here from interviews I have done with pupils about whether they have opportunities to do work that really makes them think (see Myatt 2015); from the responses from the RE Quality Mark, which checks the extent to which pupils have demanding work; and from the RE for REal project. The overall judgement on this is that pupils enjoy having work that stretches them and makes them think. One example of this: In an interview with high-prior-attaining Year 9 pupils, they were asked about the subjects that expected them to do ambitious work. In this example, they cited two subjects – Geography and Religious Education. When asked why they were made to think hard in these subjects, these were their responses: they were expected to use technical terms accurately and were regularly tested on these; their teachers did not accept one-word answers, but instead insisted on full sentences with reasoning and using the correct vocabulary; these responses were then checked with other pupils to find out whether they agreed or disagreed; all answers had to be justified with reasons, which could be challenged; and for homework they were often given news or academic articles that related to the subject – they were expected to read these and to come back with ideas and responses for the start of the next lesson. What was interesting about this discussion was that they relished the challenge, and knew that they were being stretched and treated as high-functioning thinkers and researchers. What is also interesting from a teacher's point of view is that all this takes less time – the thought that goes into the planning is to provide some interesting material, which is then discussed and debated in the next lesson. This richness has an impact on the writing or other product as a result; and it is in this that there is evidence of pupils' progress – the originality and complexity of their responses both oral and written. Shallow work simply does not provide the space for this to happen.

These pupils' responses, all made in schools that have been awarded the RE Quality Mark (Myatt 2015), show there is a hunger for deep, complex stuff with which they can engage:

- 'We get the chance to talk about what people believe and why they believe.'

- 'We understand that people might have different views from our own, even within our own traditions. It opens our eyes.'

- 'We know that beliefs and values sit behind our actions; so, we get the chance to look at some of the things which help people make decisions. In our lessons on Judaism we have been reading the Talmud, the commentary on the Torah.'

- 'It's great meeting people from different faiths. We have been to the Gurdwara where one of the members told us about some of the things he found difficult to believe in.

He said how was it possible for Guru Nanak to disappear under water for three days? Could this be true? He found it hard to believe, but went on to say that it didn't affect his faith. This was so interesting because it made us realise that plenty of people question their faith.'

- 'We have to think really hard in RE. And these discussions carry on after the lesson and even at home.'

- 'I love the connection between RS and the wider world.'

- 'RE brings religion to life.'

- 'RE is everywhere in our school; well more than that really...in RE there are no walls...'

- 'RE makes you think of questions which you might never have thought of.'

- 'In RE you get to see the rest of the world.'

- 'A big question stays with you until you find the answer.'

- 'RE is like an iceberg – as you unpack things you come to understand deeper meaning as in the parables or considering what truth means.'

- 'RE helps you to grow in maturity. Seeing the bigger picture helps you to understand things.'

In these examples, pupils are expressing a desire for complexity, for engaging with meaning and for struggling to find answers. And, interestingly, this chimes with the research from Lemov (2012), Willingham (2009) and others. It also chimes with the findings of RE for REal (Dinham and Shaw 2015), where researchers from Goldsmiths' Faiths and Civil Society Unit talked with 190 pupils in Year 10 about their views on RE. This is the summary of what they said to researchers:

- Pupils are concerned that they hear a lot of stereotypes in the media and in some of their learning. They want to know what's real.

- They think that learning about religion and belief is becoming more and more relevant because they see more of it, and what they see is more diverse.

- Almost all emphasise the role of learning about religion and belief in order to engage positively with diversity.

- Almost all emphasise the importance of learning about religion and belief to their personal development.

- Almost all want to learn about a wider range of religions and beliefs and are worried that many students learn about only one or two traditions.

- Pupils really enjoy learning about real 'lived' religion, especially through thinking about religion and belief controversies.

True challenge encourages a deeper engagement with the material; it honours the integrity of the subject domain. It is an entitlement for every pupil.

References

Brown, P., Roediger, H.L. and McDaniel, M.A. (2014) *Make It Stick: The Science of Successful Learning*. Cambridge, MA: Harvard University Press.

Dinham, A. and Shaw, M. (2015) *RE for REal: The Future of Teaching and Learning about Religion and Belief*. Accessed on 29 May 2017 via http://research.gold.ac.uk/19628

Lemov, D. (2012) *Teach Like a Champion*. Hoboken, NJ: Wiley and Uncommon Schools.

Myatt, M. (2015, 12 July) 'What students say about RE' [Blog post]. Accessed on 29 May 2017 at http://marymyatt.com/blog/2015-07-12/what-students-say-about-re

Oates, T. (2014) *National Curriculum* [Video recording]. Accessed on 29 May 2017 at www.youtube.com/watch?v=-q5vrBXFpmo

Swiss Cottage School (2015) *The Progression Puzzle*. Accessed on 29 May 2017 at www.swisscottageteachingschool.org.uk/reporting-from-the-progression-puzzle-conference

Willingham, D. (2009) *When Can You Trust the Experts?: Telling Good Science from Bad in Education*. San Francisco, CA: Jossey-Bass.

Chapter 9

PRINCIPLES AND PROCEDURES FOR CLASSROOM DIALOGUE

MIKE CASTELLI

There are four points I wish to make in this chapter: (1) Dialogue builds effective Religious Education. (2) Dialogue is a distinctive activity that is not the same as conversation or debate. (3) Dialogue needs to be taught. (4) Through the practice of the proposed principles and procedures, pupils and their teachers clarify their own thinking, their articulation of this thinking and their understanding of themselves and the other.

The nature of dialogue and its place in RE

The United Nations Education, Science and Culture Organisation (UNESCO) argues that:

> 'dialogue' derives from the Greek term 'dia-logos', widely mistranslated and wrongly understood because of a confusion between 'duo' and 'dia'. It does not mean a conversation between two persons or two groups, but an acceptance, by two participants or more, that they will compare and contrast their respective arguments. The prefix 'dia-' is equivalent to the Latin 'trans-', connoting a considerable shift in space, time, substance or thought. Dialogue is not designed to lead to a definitive conclusion. It is a constantly-renewed means of

re-initiating the thinking process, of questioning certainties, and of progressing from discovery to discovery. (UNESCO 2013, p.14)

To clarify further the definition proposed by UNESCO: dialogue needs at least two participants, self and another, and therefore this activity is not a solo activity of amassing knowledge. Knowledge is essential, but dialogue asks the pupils to place that knowledge in a specific context in order to use it to engage with the other who resides within this context. When the context is Religious Education, the ability to apply this knowledge to a specific context of the beliefs and practices of specific individuals and real communities demands a developing religious literacy and oracy: literacy to frame the question, and oracy to ask the question in a manner that opens a dialogue.

The Three Faiths Forum (n.d.) identifies 'oops' and 'ouch' questions, the premise being that a pupil can ask any question they wish of a dialogue partner, but how the question is framed demands a growing sophistication on the part of the questioner: a developing religious literacy and oracy that avoids confrontation, hurt or embarrassment. Furthermore, the knowledge underpinning such a literacy and oracy is not generic knowledge of a religious tradition, but a contextualised knowledge that reveals a specific individual within a specific community.

Good RE goes for depth rather than breadth, is contemporary and always allows the first-person voice to be heard. This voice can be heard from a pupil peer who is willing and well prepared, from a DVD or online case study, from a class visitor, in a visit to a place of worship, or in any way that ensures the knowledge learned is context-specific rather than generic. I would argue for depth rather than breadth because Religious Education aims to help pupils understand what it means to be an individual who holds specific beliefs and follows specific practices in a specific context. Religious Education cannot and should not try to teach pupils everything about a particular belief and its practices, but can, through depth rather than breadth, offer a meaningful insight into what it means to be this other in their own context. Religious Education plays its role in helping pupils understand themselves and their place in the world, therefore RE is contemporary and is about today's people. My argument is that dialogue can make a significant contribution to Religious Education; but for dialogue to be possible, pupils need to hear and respond to the first-person voice of the other, and attend to their response.

Classroom dialogue

Dialogue is frequently suggested as a positive means of exchange and learning. Alexander (2006) proposes a dialogical classroom in which teacher and pupils share the learning and teaching and where there is reciprocity in classroom talk and in the relationships between pupils and between the pupils and their teacher. A prerequisite for such reciprocity is a willingness on all parts.

> Dialogue requires a willingness and skill to engage with minds, ideas and ways of thinking other than our own; it involves the ability to question, listen, reflect, reason, explain, speculate and explore ideas; to analyse problems, form hypotheses and develop solutions; to discuss, argue, examine evidence, defend, probe, and assess arguments. (Alexander 2006, p.5)

The usefulness of dialogue in religious and belief education is also one of the findings in the Religion in Education: Contribution to Dialogue (REDCo, 2006–2009) project:

> Dialogue is a favoured strategy for teachers to cope with diversity in the classroom but students are more ambivalent; not all students are comfortable with the way diversity is managed in schools. (Weisse 2011, p.113)

REDCo was a European-Council-funded project that ran for three years with a focus on Religious Education for 14- to

16-year-old pupils in Germany, England, France, Netherlands, Estonia, Russia and Spain. The field research included interviews with pupils, teachers and parents and identified dialogue as a favoured classroom strategy.

UNESCO offers a definition of dialogue; Alexander proposes the necessary classroom dispositions and learning consequences of dialogue; teachers in the REDCo field research identify dialogue as a favoured classroom strategy. These are inspiring recommendations for classroom dialogue but is it necessary to teach pupils how to dialogue, and, if so, then how do we teach it? I have argued (Castelli 2012, 2015) that dialogue is not necessarily a disposition or set of skills pupils pick up naturally. Pupils encounter debate, confrontation and competition constantly. They only have to look at the ergonomics of the Westminster parliament, the adversarial nature of the British legal system and the competitive nature of our sports and panel games on television to pick up skills of debate, confrontation and competition. We need to teach pupils how to dialogue because it is so inherently different from these imbibed cultural experiences; they encounter few occasions of real dialogue in practice. The challenge is how to undertake this.

This chapter addresses dialogue within the Religious Education classroom, and within this context, I use the term 'belief' to include both religious and non-religious belief. I would argue that this 'belief' is manifest in those symbols and images that are important to us and that we express through our actions and avoidances. Through Religious Education pupils and teachers develop their knowledge and understanding of this belief as it is manifest in self and in others. Dialogue can be a means of achieving this. The development and practice of such dialogue applies equally to the teacher and to their pupils for two reasons: the dispositions and procedures for dialogue need to be apparent in teacher as well as pupil practices; and learning is a life-long undertaking in which teachers will also be open to learning through dialogue in their classrooms.

Teaching dialogue

I propose five dispositions and procedures that can be taught in the classroom. The exercise of these will result in pupils and their teachers practising dialogue. These are:

- Humility

- Seriousness

- Hesitation

- Imagination

- Articulation.

Humility

We infrequently encounter an encouragement to humility. Self-assurance and self-belief are the foundations for self-respect and a developing self-confidence, all of which might seem to make any call for humility slightly out of kilter with contemporary ideas of self-development. It is my argument that humility, in the context of dialogue, is a willingness to listen to and learn from another without laying aside one's own beliefs. Dialogue calls for humility because each participant comes to the other's and their own beliefs recognising that the ownership of truth is contested and partial, and that claiming a monopoly of truth makes dialogue redundant.

In his development of an understanding of dialogue, Bakhtin (1984) challenges the assumption that, if two people disagree, at least one of them must be in error. For Bakhtin, truth needs a multitude of carrying voices. It cannot be held within a single mind; it also cannot be expressed by 'a single mouth'. Truth requires many simultaneous voices. Bakhtin does not say that many voices carry partial truths that complement each other. A number of different voices do not make the truth simply 'averaged' or 'synthesised'. It is the fact of mutual addressivity, of engagement and of commitment to the context of a real-life event that distinguishes truth from untruth. Even in the best-organised debates, one party is defending a proposition they hold to be true against their opponent. In a dialogue, both parties hold a specific position but are seeking a better understanding of that of the other and are open to the possibility of a change in their own. In my proposition, I call this disposition 'humility'. Facing another with humility does not obfuscate the search for truth or encourage a tolerance of all opinions; it is an openness to the possibility of learning something of who the other is, and of challenging this, as well as an openness to the possibility of change in one's own position.

Seriousness

The ability to articulate our belief, and to learn how to dialogue with the belief of another, is a serious business because it touches on each other's meaning-making which is itself a serious undertaking.

> The point though is that to put somebody in touch with what is most serious in them, and for them, is a crucial aspiration and that is why Religious Education is not marginal, a Cinderella interest in education overall. (Williams 2005)

Helping pupils accept such seriousness also brings the type of respect to the classroom that builds pupils' confidence in developing their self-expression as they struggle to articulate personal beliefs and understandings that may often be partial and not yet fully formed. This approach to seriousness does not mean that all my opinions are given serious weighting because they are my own, but that all attempts at expressing these ideas will be treated with equal seriousness. It is in this atmosphere of seriousness and respect that the challenge that is central to dialogue can take place: my challenge to the other and their challenge to me. Alexander (2006) recognises that when such practices permeate the classroom there are social and moral consequences as 'dialogue within the classroom lays the foundation not just of successful learning, but also of social cohesion, active citizenship and good society' (p.5).

Hesitation

Hesitation is a procedure in dialogue that reflects an appreciation that belief development and belief formation is a life-long process and therefore perceptions and impressions are always partial and frequently contingent.

> I think it is about the habit of not rushing to judgement. I think that's a profoundly spiritual issue. What is it that educates in the habit of not rushing to judgement? Whether judgement of a person, or judgement about a situation? What is it that instils in us the necessary inner quiet that means we act rather than react? And somewhere in there is the very heart of the moral as well as the spiritual dimension. (Williams 2005)

Developing procedures of hesitation in the classroom asks pupils to think before they react or speak. We know that giving pupils time to think before answering a question develops their thinking skills and enhances the quality of their responses. In an atmosphere of humility and seriousness such hesitation contributes to the possibility of building a dialogical classroom where deep thinking about self and the other encourages a quality of Religious Education that builds self-understanding and an appreciation of the different other.

Imagination

In his 1845 essay on the history of the development of Christian doctrine, John Henry Newman found a key role for imagination (see Cornwell 2010, p.86). He believed that faith (belief) as an imaginative process is awakened and shaped by the images, symbols, rituals and conceptual representations of religion. Similarly, in articulating belief, pupils' literacy is enriched by an understanding and use of image, symbol, ritual and representation. The imagination to manipulate image and symbol in self-expression can also help us understand their meaning for another. Ricoeur (1992) argues that each of us is in a constant process of constructing our autobiographical self-identity through our interaction with each encounter we have, either in reality or through fiction. These encounters with individuals, groups or situations either affirm or challenge our understanding of ourselves as we identify with or reject these encounters. Ricoeur goes on to claim:

> Self-understanding is an interpretation; interpretation of the self in turn finds in the narrative, among other subjects and symbols, a privileged form of mediation; the latter borrows from history as well as from fiction, making life story a fictional history or, if one prefers, a historical fiction, interweaving the historiographic style of biographies with the novelistic style of imaginary autobiographies. (p.114)

In the dialogical classroom, imagination works alongside humility, seriousness and hesitation in placing the pupil and the teacher in the 'shoes' of the other and encourages deep thinking about the role of symbols, image and ritual in the life of self as a means of expressing our understanding of belief and practice. Symbols, images and rituals abound within pupils' experiences, but it calls for imagination to recognise their significance, be it a team flag or a Sikh khanda, Bilbo Baggins or the biblical Good Shepherd, the New Zealand haka or lighting shabbat candles.

Articulation

The ability to articulate what has been learned, and what questions arise from the learning, needs the language and skills to communicate with clarity and sensitivity, in order to develop a literacy and oracy apposite for a Religious Education classroom. Gates (2007) argues that this is teaching pupils how to be literate in religion and belief.

> The inter-subjective checks on the internal coherence of
> faith are as important to a religious tradition as to any group
> of natural scientists... From an educational point of view,
> the opportunity to check these credentials against personal
> experience is a very proper activity...to distinguish between
> encouraging children to become religious and enabling them
> to discover for themselves what it might mean to be a believer
> or an atheist – enabling them to become 'religiate', to coin a
> term. (p.18)

Gates coined the term 'religiate' more than 30 years ago, to sit
alongside 'literate' as used when teaching English and 'numerate'
when teaching mathematics. 'Religiate' is an expression of
competence in the use of knowledge and understanding
appropriate to Religious Education. The preferred term
'religious literacy' appears in several chapters in this book and
I have used the dual term of 'literacy and oracy' in this chapter.
Whichever is the preferred term, it matters that the ability to
articulate, in writing and in speech, appropriate expressions of
Religious Education should be a measure of progress in learning
about self and another. As I have argued above, dialogue is
an encounter between self and another, and central to this
encounter is not only a knowledge and understanding of the
other but also an ability to find the eloquence to question and
challenge them. The development of such eloquence results in
a refinement and further articulation of my own position. This
requires of us sensitivity as we approach the other and helps
us to think how prepared our own position is to be receptive
to these same responses. In the dialogical classroom, such
articulation is indispensable and is enhanced by predispositions
of hesitation, humility, seriousness and imagination.

Procedures

Unlike Bloom's (1956) taxonomy, there is neither a hierarchy
of value within my proposed principles and procedures of

dialogue, nor a linear sequencing of development; yet, similar to his taxonomy, dialogue demands higher-order thinking in the use of Bloom's skills of understanding, application, analysis, synthesis and evaluation. These dialogue procedures are cyclical. The learning and teaching process may be entered at any point within the cycle determined by the focus of the study, the learning outcome of the teaching plan and the learning needs of the pupils. Dialogue is at the heart of this proposed educational enterprise. Alexander argues that learning through dialogue stands in opposition to that one-sided and cognitively undemanding interaction that has been exposed consistently, by classroom research, where the teacher asks questions to which he or she knows the answers; the pupils dutifully spot or guess those answers and recognise that what they, as pupils, say carries authority only if the teacher allows it to do so. Bloom's higher-order skills cannot thrive in a teacher-centred and teacher-controlled learning environment. Dialogue presumes a greater degree of reciprocity in classroom talk and relationships and lays the foundation not just of successful learning, but, as I have noted from Alexander above, also of social cohesion, active citizenship and good society. The argument is that the development of pupils' ability to dialogue both complements and contradicts their ubiquitous experiences of debate, competition and confrontation. In a contemporary world where religion and belief frequently elicit responses of aggression and violence, dialogue offers an alternative response and may obviate the recourse to conflict. Furthermore, the development of the ability to dialogue in the proposed manner empowers individuals by affirming their role in their own learning because, as Dewey (1938) explains:

> There is, I think, no point in the philosophy of progressive education which is sounder than its emphasis upon the importance of the participation of the learner in the formation of the purpose which directs his activities in the learning process... (p.269)

Dialogue, RE and conflict

The association between religion and conflict cannot be ignored. Conflict can be addressed through the teaching and practice of dialogue in the classroom, and beyond; this can be a means by which pupils 'learn about religious diversity' and are then able 'to have conversations about religion/belief' (Weisse 2011). More than this, they will develop the skills to have a conversation that results in tolerance of the different other; and even more, a conversation that can lead to dialogue at a level where differences as well as similarities, challenges as well as complements, are exchanged in a manner which does not lead to hurt or violence. It is for this reason that dialogue is antithetical to conflict. Within the RE classroom, the skills of dialogue not only promote understanding but also develop each participant's ability to articulate their own belief or explain their own practices in dialogue with another. Such a proposed dialogue is dynamic in Ricoeur's (1992) dialectical sense, as self is revealed through the encounter with other-than-self. The ability to articulate something of our self-awareness and respond to that of another is a dialectic that clarifies and refines perceptions of self and other.

Bauman's (1996, p.26) image of contemporary culture as a 'jamming session' has much in common with the dialogical classroom. When jamming, a musician hears, interprets and responds to the other participants in the session. In responding, the musician may challenge and change the direction of the music but remains a participant, sometimes solo and other times in polyphony. Our classrooms could be enriched if all participants experienced them as jamming sessions.

References

Alexander, R. (2006) *Education as Dialogue: Moral and Pedagogical Choices for a Runaway World*. Hong Kong: Hong Kong Institute of Education.

Bakhtin, M. (1984) *Problems of Dostoevsky's Poetics* (C. Emerson, ed. and transl.). Minneapolis, MN: University of Minnesota Press.

Bauman, G. (1996) *Contesting Cultures: Discourses in Multi-ethnic London.* Cambridge: Cambridge University Press.

Bloom, B. (ed.) (1956) *Taxonomy of Educational Objectives: Handbook 1. Cognitive Domain.* London: Longman Green.

Castelli, M. (2012) 'Faith dialogue as a pedagogy for a post-secular religious education.' *Journal of Beliefs and Values 33*, 2, 207–216.

Castelli, M. (2015) 'Dialogue skills for religious education.' *Ricerche Di Pedagogia e Didattica [Journal of Theories and Research in Education] 10*, 1, 151–167.

Cornwell, J. (2010) *Newman's Unquiet Grave.* London: Continuum.

Dewey, J. (1938) *Experience and Education.* New York, NY: Simon and Schuster.

Gates, B. (2007) *Transforming Religious Education.* London: Bloomsbury Publishing.

Ricoeur, P. (1992) *Oneself as Other.* Chicago, IL: University of Chicago Press.

Three Faiths Forum (n.d.) *Interfaith Rules and Tools.* Accessed on 25 June 2017 at www.3ff.org.uk/ resources/rules-and-tools.php#language

UNESCO (2013) *Intercultural Competences: Conceptual and Operational Framework.* Paris: UNESCO.

Weisse, W. (2011) 'Reflections on REDCo project.' *British Journal of Religious Education 33*, 2, 111–125.

Williams, R. (2005, May). Unpublished address to the Religious Education Council of England and Wales.

Chapter 10

FACING THE STRANGE

PHIL CHAMPAIN

This chapter argues that Religious Education can be a safe space for discussing unsafe ideas. In doing so, the author first explores what we mean by 'unsafe ideas' and 'safe space' in today's society, before outlining how concern for both has shaped education policy. This then sets up a discussion about the kinds of classroom approaches that are both necessary and practically possible for the effective handling of unsafe ideas in RE. At the heart of this chapter is the argument that RE, more than other subjects, offers the potential to explore personal expressions of faith, belief and identity. It is this exploration of lived experience of faith and belief that can, with careful facilitation, lead to the discussion of ideas that may be deemed 'unsafe'. The chapter concludes by underlining the importance of handling controversy and disagreement in school, and the role that RE can play in doing so safely.

Unsafe ideas

A new public museum opened in Palestine in May 2016. It has the motto 'A safe space for unsafe ideas'. Eighteen years in the making, this museum aims to explore Arab history, to speak about contemporary Palestine and to help see what the future might look like. Public exploration of alternative futures in this troubled part of the world is unsafe indeed. The year of 2016 is also when, at the Ayyam Gallery in Dubai, painter Shurooq Amin exhibited her new series 'Popcornographic', which aims to

155

expose the hypocrisy of attitudes towards women in her native Kuwait. More evidence of a safe space for unsafe ideas perhaps.

And in January 2016 the death of David Bowie reminded us of his impact on culture and ideas. Bowie was about posing questions, whether on identity, spirituality, gender or sexuality. We should not forget the art of challenging assumptions and stereotypes; of questioning others and more importantly learning the art of questioning ourselves; of providing ways of creating opportunities for engagement where people can, as Bowie put it in his hit 'Young Americans', 'turn and face the strange'. Challenging norms has always been a part of our makeup as human beings. It is not the purpose here to shine a light on why this continues to be the case. We are inquisitive, curious beings, and all the more so when we are growing up through school and college.

Safe space

The difficulty lies in how best to manage this exploration and challenging of ideas in ways that are constructive, yet give space for open expression in ways that do not involve resorting to violence or fuelling hatred. It is this uncertainty about where exchanging ideas will lead us that squeezes the space for discussing the very ideas that challenge the core assumptions upon which we determine which behaviour and attitudes are acceptable and which are not. And it is this uncertainty that underpins the application of policy to regulate the expression of ideas.

The author of the term 'safe space' is regarded by some commentators as Kurt Lewin, a psychologist who, in the 1940s, was asked to help develop leadership training for corporate bosses. Interestingly, Lewin was a Jewish academic who left Europe after the rise of Nazism and moved to the United States. Out of his work came the invention of 'sensitivity training', which was a form of group discussion. Staff could give honest feedback to each other to allow them to become aware of any bias in their underlying assumptions and behaviors. Practically, this meant that there was an explicit rule that everyone agreed to at the start of the group. A 'safe space' was created, confidential and free of judgement, to allow people to mention views and concerns without fear of being condemned for them, on the understanding that they were open to other perspectives. In this sense, such space needs to hold both right and responsibility – no easy task.

The impact of education policy

The challenge of holding these two principles together has surfaced of late in the 'no platforming' policies of universities (though lauded by many as an important policy, 'no platforming' has also attracted criticism for barring important viewpoints), and in the continued difficulties faced by teachers in handling controversial issues; students and teachers face challenges in handling taboo topics often because these issues can lead to emotional outbursts and interpersonal conflict. This unease with complexity and controversy does perhaps reflect a yearning for safety in a dangerous world (Daesh, immigration, rising inequality, climate change, falling confidence in politicians, Brexit, etc.), but it also risks feeding the need for protection to such an extent that we begin to identify ourselves too quickly as victims or potential victims. Rather than this, we need the opportunity, capacity and confidence to engage constructively with a range of ideas, whether deemed safe or not. This said, it is nevertheless the case that the delivery of education does not always provide us with such opportunity.

Ivan Illich (1971) would go so far as to argue that schools are tools through which ideas can be controlled. Noam Chomsky (1998) suggests that 'the smart way to keep people passive and obedient is to strictly limit the spectrum of acceptable opinion, but allow very lively debate within that spectrum' (p.43). With concern over British values, integration, community cohesion and extremism, what constitutes acceptable opinion is indeed being regulated. There are perceived good reasons for this, including the safeguarding of young people from violent extremism.

On the other hand, efforts to promote community cohesion also legitimised space for addressing hard issues relating to integration. Under the 2006 Education and Inspections Act, schools were given a duty to promote community cohesion. This required 'every school – whatever its intake and wherever it is located...[to educate] children and young people who will live and work in a country which is diverse in terms of cultures, religions, beliefs and social backgrounds (Department for Children, Schools and Families 2007, Section 1). Community cohesion was therefore included in the Ofsted framework and schools had to review how they addressed the area whilst inspectors reported on schools' practice (Trethewey and Menzies 2015).

Following the 2010 general election in the UK, the Coalition government announced a drive towards 'autonomy' for schools and introduced a slimmed-down Ofsted framework that no longer included community cohesion. Instead, the new framework emphasised 'spiritual, moral, social and cultural education' (SMSC) as the place for exploring issues of identity. Whilst increased autonomy could work both ways in terms of allowing space for exploring unsafe ideas, SMSC represented a key area of the curriculum where this could happen.

In 2014, the government introduced a new duty to promote 'British values'. The new duty aims to make pupils 'into citizens who respect difference, who welcome disagreement and who challenge intolerance' (Morgan 2015). On the face of it, this offers an opportunity for exploring different ideas and requires pupils to accept and engage with 'mutual respect and tolerance of those with different faiths and beliefs' (Ofsted 2016, p.35). Whilst the language used is different, schools are once again being required to foster understanding and tolerance.

The response to 'British values' from teachers and school leaders has been mixed however. Whilst research by

The Key (2015) suggests that over 70 percent of school leaders feel that promoting British values is an appropriate role for schools, concerns have been raised that Ofsted's approach to inspecting British values has moved the goalposts. Although many teachers welcome the opportunity to explore identity and values in schools, many are concerned that the title 'British values' implies these values are uniquely British. They fear that this could exclude other nationalities or those with more complex heritage. Managing the space for exploring faith and identity is complex.

The British government's Prevent strategy also has implications for the discussion of unsafe ideas in schools. It recommends that schools should provide a 'safe environment for discussing controversial issues'. However, this too has been greeted with concern in some corners with the National Union of Teachers 2015 Annual Conference passing a motion stating that 'many school staff are now unwilling to allow discussions in their classroom for fear of the consequences'. This reflects a fear that 'British values' and Prevent may in fact close down spaces for discussion, since the Prevent duty comes with a responsibility for teachers to report pupils who are deemed to be showing signs of radicalisation.

It seems finding the right policies to support the challenging task of handling unsafe ideas is problematic, which is itself a reflection of the complexity of the task. Whilst policy has pointed towards broad notions of encouraging community cohesion and SMSC in schools, government has been less specific about the opportunities offered by RE for handling what constitutes an acceptable 'spectrum of opinions'. At the time of writing there is a government consultation into 'Schools that Work for Everyone'. As part of this consultation, the 50 percent co-religionists cap on faith schools is under review, and the 'twinning' or linking of faith schools to improve integration is under consideration. However, there is little discussion about the role RE can play in strengthening cohesion and integration through the exploration of unsafe ideas. This is the focus of the next section, which will highlight how RE provides a place for stretching the spectrum of ideas and opinions that may be deemed 'unsafe'.

The school and classroom

Given the need to discuss 'unsafe ideas' in schools, but the unease in handling them, which leads to policies that can limit the opportunities to explore them, why does RE offer a solution? Why does the teaching of RE offer opportunities to explore unsafe ideas that other subjects do not? And how can this be done in ways that nurture citizens who respect difference, who welcome disagreement and who challenge intolerance? To understand this, we need to consider the way RE can offer space for exploring identity, in ways that other subjects are not so inclined to do, though SMSC in all subjects also offers similar space. If approached through the prism of knowledge dissemination, via books and texts, then RE is arguably limited in its ability to open up the safe exploration of unsafe ideas. Teaching from texts about different beliefs and faiths is of course valuable and important, but it is difficult to express the reality of difference and what different faiths mean to different people unless the subject can be personalised. If faith is not personalised, then there is the additional danger that generalisations about faith can in fact reinforce an 'us and them' mentality: that all Christians are the same, that all Muslims think the same, and that generic differences somehow keep us apart, or that generic ideas can bring us together. Faith and belief is complex, and it is important to embrace this notion. It also connects us to some of the most controversial issues that are of such concern to policy makers. For part of the complexity of faith is that it intersects with other dimensions of identity, with our varied needs and interests; with how we see the world and how our needs and interests can be at odds with social norms. They can be challenging to others. Personalising faith and belief can be undoubtedly difficult and uncomfortable. The personal nature of our faiths and beliefs means we make ourselves vulnerable when we reveal them to others in too much detail. Nevertheless, learning to articulate them and explain them is a powerful way of opening up dialogue that is at once challenging and educational.

Taken at face value, RE is about religious faith. I would argue, however, that in such a diverse society where 'levels of atheism stand at...20% (and)...people are less likely to associate with, or relate to, a particular religion' (Woodhead 2013, p.23), RE should also include an exploration of non-religious belief. Faith or belief is personal, so RE offers an opportunity to reach into this personal terrain, in ways that touch on identity and values. It is by engaging with our values that we can begin to challenge assumptions and begin to explore ideas that are felt to be unsafe. Given this opportunity that RE offers then, how can an exploration of lived faith and belief, and the risks this carries, be brought safely into the classroom? One approach is to train individual 'speakers' to go into classrooms and tell pupils the story of their faith or belief, how they came to embrace them and how they live them out in their everyday lives. This is an approach adopted by the interfaith organisation Three Faiths Forum (3FF). Two to three carefully trained speakers tell their stories to pupils, taking about ten minutes each. They each bring with them an object that symbolises something about their story. It is important that each speaker represents a different faith or belief. Once the stories have been told, pupils are encouraged to ask questions and begin to explore ideas. An illustration of the kinds of stories that are told can be seen below, followed by a range of questions and comments that pupils have shared in response. It is important a skilled facilitator accompanies the speakers to ensure the speakers stick to their brief and to time, and that the ensuing discussion is managed safely and effectively. A key task of the facilitator is to establish, before the class starts, a group commitment to an ethical dialogue that all pupils can invest in and share joint responsibility for, to help manage sensitivities that may arise – and this is achieved through a 'safe space' group commitment. The facilitator holds, protects and refers back to this principled framework when required.

Jewish speaker story

A Jewish speaker shares their story of being raised in a practising Orthodox Jewish family in a non-Jewish area. The story illustrates the speaker's journey through a changing relationship with faith as they grow into adulthood. The story reflects key moments, such as a gap year in Israel and the theological questions it triggers; interfaith experiences such as being president of their university's Jewish Society and vice-president of the Islamic Society; and discovering their bisexuality at university. It illustrates the negotiation between faith and sexuality, and concludes with sharing how the speaker has left behind the Jewish practice of their upbringing to define their connection with Judaism for themselves.

Christian speaker story

A Christian speaker shares their story of being raised in a family that identified as being Christian. However, aside from an occasional visit to church the family didn't practise key elements of the faith. The story journeys through a challenging period in the speaker's life through secondary school, where home life was turbulent and unpredictable, coupled with the loss of a close family member. These circumstances culminated in the speaker losing hope and purpose in his life, before a chance encounter with a new friend who invited him along to church. This led to the speaker finding purpose and acceptance within church but also an opportunity to study the Bible, ask questions and discover God on a personal level. This story illustrates the many difficulties, challenges and effects of growing up within broken homes, and the role that faith and belief can have in re-directing and renewing hope through acceptance and purpose. The speaker concludes by talking about how his faith plays out in his life now through being a pastor in a local church and supporting homeless young people in his home.

Muslim speaker story

A Muslim speaker shares her story of being of an East African origin born in the Middle East and growing up as a teenager in London. The speaker explains how she found this combination of backgrounds and new setting challenging in identifying and expressing her own identity. However, that challenge paved the way to reconnecting with the Quran, Islam's sacred book. She concludes with assuring the students that she has done well in her life because she found in her Islamic faith a source of comfort and grounding in a constantly changing world.

Questions asked by students

- 'How does your family feel about you not being religious any more?'

- 'What were the experiences that challenged you during your gap year in Israel?'

- 'How did you end up being the vice-president of the Islamic Society?'

- 'What does Judaism say about bisexuality?'

- 'Are there any practices that you observe from Judaism?'

- 'Would you change your experiences in early life or do you think they shaped who you are today?'

- 'How is your relationship with your parents?'

- 'What is your favourite story or verse in the Bible?'

- 'What is it like living with homeless young people? Are you ever worried?'

- 'Can you pray about anything?'

- 'Do you believe that Jesus was God?'

- 'What does a pastor do?'

- 'What is Grace?'

- 'How long did it take you to learn English and what did you do until then?'

- 'Did you feel lonely when you were in school in the UK?'

- 'I like your headscarf. Why do you dress the way you do?'

- 'If you were not born into a Muslim family, do you think you would have chosen Islam as your religion?'

- 'Where is home for you?'

Crafting a safe space

Classic safe space principles

- *Respect* – What does this mean? How do we as a group define and express it?

- *Active listening* – Really taking in what someone else is saying throughout, without already focusing on formulating the response in your own head.

- *Dialogue not debate* – This space is not about determining right or wrong or true or untrue, it's about sharing perspectives and understanding the stories and experiences behind them.

- *I-statements* – Always speaking on behalf of yourself, to own your words and opinions, and to avoid generalising and misrepresenting others through language.

- *Oops–Ouch* – Everyone is on a learning journey, and controversial questions come from a place of genuine curiosity or confusion. 'Oops' and 'Ouch' provide amnesty moments in the dialogue process. 'Oops' is uttered as a signal by the speaker to pause the process and rephrase their question in a more sensitive way. Similarly, the listener, when offended by the way a question has been posed, has the opportunity to say 'Ouch'. This again pauses the process, alerts the asker and gives them an opportunity to rephrase. It also provides an opportunity to explore why a particular question might be offensive.

This setting of safe space echoes the approach of Kurt Lewin described earlier. Rather than interpreting 'safe space' as free of risk, it is important to keep working at crafting the space that can hold the difficult conversations that are needed. There needs to be safe but also robust space where risks can be taken and where we can chip away at taboos. Exploration of individual, lived faith and belief within RE takes us in this direction. We should not expect our pupils to readily tell their own stories, but we can expose them in a safe way to the stories of others and accompany them on a journey of exploration. Of course, this can lead to penetrating and uncomfortable questions and responses (see questions above), but these are exactly the questions we need to begin to challenge assumptions and deepen our understanding of different faiths and beliefs.

Teaching strategies

The teacher as facilitator also needs to have the competency to handle controversial issues in the classroom. This competency goes beyond ground rules for managing safe space, though this is an important part of it. 3FF have developed a workshop that supports pupils to ask difficult questions. This 'Art of Asking' approach requires careful facilitation to deal with students' reactions to what they have heard so that they can critically unpack the meaning behind any questions they may wish to ask. Students explore the power of language, asking sensitive questions, and investigate how language can be helpful or unhelpful for opening dialogue and creating understanding between people of different beliefs. In another workshop, 'The Art of Empathy', students consider assumptions people make about them and their classmates based on how they look; they explore the concept of complex identities, and practise tools and techniques for going beyond face-value and activating empathy towards others. These are two workshops that can help students handle controversial issues. Training teachers of RE in these approaches will enhance the effectiveness of RE in handling unsafe ideas. These workshops and approaches provide an encounter pupils would not normally experience. The process plants a seed that for some will develop further questions and enquiry about faith, belief and identity. More sustained and extended support to teachers will help produce more fruit, and this can come in a number of forms.

There are 3FF training packages for teachers, such as 'Faith, Belief and Identity in the Classroom' where teachers learn strategies for building and maintaining a safe and supportive environment for dialogue about faith, belief and identity within their classrooms. The training provides practical tools for exploration and creative activity development. It builds teachers' personal skills for sensitive and effective communication in this context. The 3FF training involved in 'Dealing with Controversial Issues' focuses on providing practical tools for transforming challenging moments into positive learning experiences for students. Teachers have an opportunity to practise skills for remaining calm and taking positive action during difficult discussions. The School Linking Network (SLN) and 3FF both run linking programmes bringing schools together, something that has a particular appeal and relevance in the context of this chapter. Nurturing the seeds that may be planted through one-off encounter sessions is clearly important and demands collaborative approaches between schools and agencies providing these opportunities and methodologies that can help create safe spaces for exploring unsafe ides, such as those provided by SLN and 3FF. Any subsequent inter-school collaboration needs to be driven by senior management within schools, and can also be championed by local authorities.

Conclusion

Whilst the importance of protection from irresponsible and potentially harmful opinion and propaganda must be recognised, we need to remain confident that we have and can build the skills to handle controversy and disagreement. How else can we work through and with complexity? How else can we understand those different to ourselves? How else can we understand our own assumptions and biases, and responsibly challenge those of others? How else can we generate new knowledge?

RE offers a space for this to happen in schools. However, some important ingredients need to be present if it is to be effective. By focusing on people's lived experience of faith and belief, RE can help challenge simplistic labels that compartmentalise us into distinct groups. As one teacher explains:

> Some of our children live their lives without meeting someone from another culture until they go to high school or even the workplace. They can grow up with such a lot of misconceptions and prejudices... Our pupils think it's amazing that they [white kids] like pizza too. (Trethewey and Menzies 2015, p.6)

This focus on lived faith and belief needs to be accompanied by the setting and management of a 'safe space' in which pupils can be supported to ask and respond to difficult questions. And teachers need support in how to handle controversial questions and discussion in the classroom. The recent Commission on Religion and Belief in British Public Life made the point that:

> Education about religion and belief is essential because it is in schools and colleges that there is the best and earliest chance of breaking down ignorance and developing individuals who

will be receptive to the other and to ask difficult questions without fear of offending. (Commission on Religion and Belief in British Public Life 2015, p.36)

This is no easy task, but with the right skills and approaches, RE can deliver one of the most important aspects of education: helping pupils engage critically with some of the most difficult issues that they encounter in contemporary society. This is because RE offers, arguably more than any other subject, the opportunity for pupils to explore who they are as individuals, what they think and how they view the world, and how they articulate faith, belief, values and the meaning they give to their lives.

References

Chomsky, N. (1998) *The Common Good*. Berkeley, CA: Odonian Press.

Commission on Religion and Belief in British Public Life (2015) *Living with Difference: Community, Diversity and the Common Good*. Accessed on 25 May 2017 at www.woolf.cam.ac.uk/uploads/LivingwithDifference.pdf

Department for Children, Schools and Families (2007) *Guidance on the Duty to Promote Community Cohesion*. London: DCSF.

Illich, I. (1971) *De-schooling Society*. London: Calder and Boyers.

Morgan, N. (2015) *Why Knowledge Matters*. Secretary of State's Winter Address to Politeia. Accessed on 29 May 2017 at www.gov.uk/government/speeches/nicky-morgan-why-knowledge-matters

Ofsted (2016) *School Inspection Handbook*. Accessed on 29 May 2017 at www.gov.uk/government/publications/school-inspection-handbook-from-september-2015

The Key (2015) *State Education: Survey Report*. Accessed on 11 December 2016 at www.thekeysupport.com/State-of-Education-2015

Trethewey, A. and Menzies, L. (2015) *Encountering Faith and Beliefs*. London: 3FF and LKMco.

Woodhead, L. (2013) *British Social Attitudes Report Finds Trust in Freefall*. London: The Conversation Trust (UK).

Chapter 11

RELIGIOUS EDUCATION AS A SAFE SPACE FOR DISCUSSING UNSAFE IDEAS

NEIL McKAIN

When does free speech become offensive speech? Does the tolerance of others impede the search for truth? Are there no right answers in RE, but only the expression of personal opinions? These are foundational challenges facing RE teachers every day, and this chapter faces them head on; it offers some ways forward through an examination of an appropriate philosophy of education and a set of classroom ground rules that can help teachers develop students' skills in recognising the dilemmas these questions pose and strategies for engaging with them.

Introduction

Thinkers as diverse as Mill and Dawkins have challenged the practice of ring-fencing received ideas:

> The beliefs which we have most warrant for, have no safeguard to rest on, but a standing invitation to the whole world to prove them unfounded. (John Stuart Mill 1859/1974, p.81)

> Nothing should be off limits to discussion. No, let me amend that. If you think some things should be off limits, let's sit down together and discuss that proposition itself. (Richard Dawkins 2014)

Safe spaces, trigger warnings, snowflakes, no-platforming, trolling: the postmodern lexicon surrounding free speech has grown so much over recent years that it now requires its own dictionary. The rise of 'safe space' culture in higher education in America has begun to permeate university campuses in the UK (Hillman 2016), and we would be naive to think that this has not had a trickle-down effect on schools. In a recent A Level lesson, I set my students the following question: 'Is Augustine right to argue that all human beings are born sinful?' Someone replied very firmly and directly 'No', giving the justification that Adam and Eve are mythological beings and so we cannot inherit anything from them. That individual then stopped and said, very contritely, that they did not mean to offend anyone, before asking, 'Are there any creationists in here?' Perhaps this has always been the case. Perhaps this is a positive sign that students do not wish to belittle the beliefs of others. But how should we as RE teachers deal with this fear of causing offence? How do we train students to be robust in defending their arguments and ideas? Are we tying our hands behind our backs if we try to do so in an RE classroom that has been designated as a 'safe space'?

What do students think about freedom of speech in the RE classroom?

Recent research into students' experiences of RE highlighted that, for many, a core justification for the subject was that it provided a safe space to share opinions and ideas. The 2015 RE for REal report (Dinham and Shaw 2015) offered conclusions on the future of RE drawn from interviews with teachers, parents, employers and students. The responses related to freedom of speech are interesting. The authors concluded: 'whether in inner city or more rural schools, students are concerned about not offending others. They feel RE should help them to manage difference positively and avoid offence' (p.8). They quote one student who said:

It's for our future as well, because if you're not used to being around them sort of people now...when you're older and working and you come across one of them, you know what to say and what not to say...so you don't accidentally say something they could be offended by. (p.11)

Now I am convinced that none of us would want to cause offence, either intentionally or accidentally, through ignorance, but should RE encourage this way of thinking? Fox (2016) makes the counter-argument that fear of causing offence stifles truth and is a threat, both to the mission of the Academy and, ultimately, to democracy itself. A teacher quoted in the RE for REal report makes the following statement:

I think RE is that safe environment where they can ask questions, is it ok to use the word 'black?' Am I ok to use this word? And you say; 'No, it's definitely not', and you talk about why. It's a safe environment for them to think, 'right that's why I'm not allowed to say that and that's why it's bad and there is a consequence'. I really worry that if RE is not part of the curriculum there is no other subject that would allow the kids to do that. That really does concern me. (p.16)

Obviously, we are unaware of the context of this specific example, but it is the underlying principle that most concerns me. If we raise a generation of children whose primary concern is not to cause offence, and who rely upon their RE teacher as an arbiter of what is acceptable to say, rather than learning to criticise ideas and seek the truth, then have we lost sight of what education is for?

No right answers in RE?

I see another, more insipid, cause of this concern not to cause offence. This is what I call the 'no right answer' problem. I have lost track of the number of times I have heard RE teachers say that the subject is special and different because there are no right answers. I have heard RE teachers enthusiastically welcome (rather than challenge) similar comments from parents that the subject is great because children get to share their opinions without fear of being told they are wrong. Perhaps the positive here is that this approach could lead to a meaningful and critical search for truth. An excellent example of this approach is the free online Justice course where the Harvard University philosopher Michael Sandel adopts the Socratic method in teaching politics and ethics to his students. But notice the key word, 'truth'. Socrates was not a relativist. Sandel is not one either. The idea that in RE there are no right answers leads to people claiming their classrooms as safe spaces where all ideas are equal and all opinions, no matter how vacuous or ill-informed, are valid. Time and time again the RE for REal report quotes students who see RE as being all about opinions:

- 'I think RE is good just to say what you feel...to speak your mind in a way that you can't be judged...' (p.12)

- 'RS is the only subject you get to express your opinion.' (p.12)

- 'By debating things in class and other opinions it means you are more accepting about other opinions and views when you go out into the world...so you don't end up offending people...' (p.11)

- 'Quite often we're not really looking at religion. It's just different opinions.' (p.14)

Teachers who defend this 'no-right-answers' model as a way of promoting tolerance and freedom of speech in fact end up with the opposite. Students think they are learning tolerance and not to cause offence, but in fact they are not being given the intellectual knowledge and tools to criticise ideas and beliefs they think are wrong; and teachers find they are unable to say that students are wrong about anything, as the students will quite rightly respond (and, as I have had thrown back at me),

'I thought there was no right or wrong answer in RE: it's about my opinion.' The reformed GCSE specifications require a moving-away from personal opinion to a more 'academic' evaluation. It is a real opportunity for students to be taught key aspects of critical thinking like reliability of sources, hermeneutics, logical contradictions and confirmation bias; otherwise, it remains likely that awarding organisations, and therefore RE teachers, will continue to fall back on allowing students to use 'I think' or 'My opinion is', which brings the answer back to a subjective judgement rather than a conclusion based on logical reasoning.

Is RE special?

Many of the ideas we discuss in a broad RE curriculum can be highly contentious. Teaching a multiplicity of faiths and the history of religious belief systems can lead to students experiencing challenges to the faith in which they have been fostered. Discussing and debating complex moral issues such as the role of women in religion or the relationship between religion and terrorism can provoke strong personal reactions from students and vociferous arguments on all sides. Many will say this is what makes RE such an important subject. As the student quoted above argues, 'RE is the only subject where you get to express your opinion'. Really? Do we believe that? Even if true, is that a foundation on which to base the future of the subject? From experience of teaching in a number of different types of school, students are free and willing to express their opinions across the curriculum. Students debate euthanasia and the death penalty in English classes and discuss genocide and nuclear weapons in History. They debate issues of unfair trade and globalisation in Geography. We can of course throw PSHE and Citizenship into the mix too. Are we mistaken in the widely held view that RE is the 'only' or the 'best' space to discuss unsafe ideas?

Another key finding of the RE for REal research was that respondents felt that good RE can play a leading role in community cohesion – not just in school but in wider society. The authors of the report do clearly say that RE has been colonised by issues such as citizenship and community cohesion and that these have blurred what the subject is about and are not a basis on which to build its future. At a recent event entitled 'Religion: From enlightenment toleration to 21st century offence', I proposed that you cannot expect or demand respect and tolerance when one side is ignorant of the history, ideology, beliefs and practices of others. I asked the audience, adults as well as current students, whether they felt their RE throughout their schooling had prepared them well enough to understand religion in the world today. Zero hands were raised. We as a subject community clearly have a lot of work to do. And yet some of us feel our hands are tied. Fear of causing offence is not the only issue we face.

RE and preventing extremism

Many teachers, particularly those of RE, are fearful that the Prevent agenda, and subsequent legislation requiring schools to detect and report students at risk of 'extremism', pose a real risk to freedom of expression in classrooms. In September 2015, the then Prime Minister, David Cameron, released a statement in defence of the new statutory obligations that public institutions were under, with regard to preventing extremism:

> It is not about oppressing [sic] free speech or stifling academic freedom, it is about making sure that radical views and ideas are not given the oxygen they need to flourish. Schools, universities and colleges, more than anywhere else, have a duty to protect impressionable young minds and ensure that our young people are given every opportunity to reach their potential. (Prime Minister's Office 2015)

The published advice from the government (Department for Education 2015) contains the following reference again to that term 'safe space':

> Schools should provide a safe space in which children, young people and staff can understand the risks associated with terrorism and develop the knowledge and skills to be able to challenge extremist arguments.

But what is an extremist? How do teachers identify extremist views? The definition given by the government in the same statutory guidance states:

> Extremism is vocal or active opposition to fundamental British values, including democracy, the rule of law, individual liberty and mutual respect and tolerance of different faiths and beliefs.

As highlighted by RE teachers such as Andrew Lewis (2015) and commentators such as Owen Jones (2015), this is a highly problematic definition that can in fact stifle debate. For example, how does an RE teacher deal with the fact that the Archbishop of Canterbury, Justin Welby (2016), gave an address in which he related this conversation with an unnamed senior politician?

> The 'very senior politician' said, 'Are you seriously going to tell me that I don't call someone an extremist if they say that their faith is more important than the rule of law?' So I [Welby] took a deep breath and said 'Well, you've got a real problem here because for me personally my faith is more important than the rule of law, so, you've got an extremist sitting in here with you... We do not believe as Christians that the rule of law outweighs everything else, we believe that the kingdom of God outweighs everything else.

Replace the word 'Christians' with 'Muslims' and replace 'kingdom of God' with 'Sharia law' and you see why many RE teachers are rightly suspicious of the efficacy and utility of the Prevent strategy. Whilst no responsible adult working in schools would shirk their duty of care towards the young people in their charge, how should we react to comments made by students that are deemed radical and extreme? If a Muslim or Christian student says that their faith matters more to them than the rule of law, do we ring up the Home Office? If a student says that circumcision is child abuse and should be outlawed, does that not go against the definition of mutual respect and tolerance of different faiths? Young people often do make such comments. Indeed, the well-trained and experienced RE teacher may even want to encourage them to do so by playing the role of devil's advocate with a desire to challenge their ideas and develop their understanding. If an RE teacher wishes students to learn about the history of art in Islam by showing 14th century devotional Persian images of Muhammad are they also at risk of causing offence and undermining mutual respect and tolerance? If, when wanting to teach students about iconoclasm and freedom of speech, an RE teacher uses the Charlie Hebdo cartoons of Muhammad, is this in line with fundamental British values? Despite reassurances from the government, to do so, in both cases, might be potentially dangerous for the teacher and school involved. As we have seen, the idea that the RE classroom can even be considered a safe space at all is not as straightforward a notion as may first appear.

Philosophy of education

While RE teachers in a senior school setting will likely cover freedom of speech when teaching about religion in the media, freedom of speech remains an under-represented subject in the philosophy of education. The late Professor Roy Harris (2009) argues that this is most likely down to the fact that educational theorists have primarily adopted a Platonic model of education, where freedom of speech is superseded by other values. How much primacy should be given to freedom of speech? Is it a tool with which one can achieve a higher good? What is that higher good? It is outside the boundaries of this chapter to argue about the aims and purposes of RE. Enough ink has been wasted on that particular question to fill the world's oceans. Harris does though propose an interesting thesis which argues that how you see the issue of freedom of speech as impacting on education will depend on which of three models of education you adopt. He classifies these as Socratic, Platonic and Aristotelian. The article is brief but fascinating, and certainly worth reading. In the space available I will set out one of the three positions Harris draws and how it relates to the issues so far discussed.

Harris argues that Socrates is primarily a dialogic teacher. He famously refused to write anything down, and from what we know he taught through oral argument in public. Harris writes: 'What marks Socrates's thinking is a supreme indifference to society and social values. He just didn't care what other people thought of his teachings' (2009, p.121). The implication here is that the best teachers are those prepared to take the greatest risks and ask the most difficult questions. But look what happened to Socrates at the end! No wonder teachers are scared of discussing potentially unsafe issues in the classroom. They fear they will be charged with corrupting the youth of Athens. Harris argues:

> Fundamental to the Socratic view of education is that you have to learn how to value your own beliefs and be prepared to defend them. It's no good just proclaiming 'I believe this' or 'I believe that' and letting the matter rest there. That is not a mark of education but of pig-headedness. (p.122)

Socrates would certainly dismiss the views of those who see RE as being all about opinions. The problem remains though of how we educate students so that they can learn to justify their various claims to truth.

Ground rules

Professor Bob Jackson (2014) has made recommendations for Council of Europe member states to adopt and implement in the area of Religious Education. Chapter 5 is of particular interest to us as it is entitled 'The Classroom as a Safe Space'. Can Jackson, with his wealth of experience, expertise and research, provide us with some useful context in dealing with the issues surrounding freedom of speech in RE and some solutions to these issues? Jackson's research leads to a focus on what he terms 'dialogic learning'. This owes much to the tradition established by Socrates and expertly exemplified by Michael Sandel. In order for this to work, the teacher must be aware of their own power and position in the dynamic of the classroom, and in Jackson's words adopt 'an impartial procedural position' (p.55). Whether this position of impartiality is ever possible is not within the scope of this chapter, but what we do see highlighted is that when thinking about freedom of speech in the classroom, what we must consider (and I would argue value and promote) is the position, power, experience and knowledge of the teacher. I shall return to this at the end of the chapter whilst looking at possible solutions and strategies when discussing unsafe ideas in the classroom.

Jackson goes on to posit a set of ground rules that establish a safe space in the classroom. They include seemingly obvious ones that any teacher trying to instil respect and good behaviour would apply, such as only using appropriate language, listening to others carefully, only having one person speak at a time, etc. They also include some specific rules tied to the ideas being discussed in this chapter. These are first that 'respect should be shown for the right of others to express views and beliefs different from one's own', and second that 'ideas should be challenged, not the individuals who express them' (Jackson 2014, p.56).

These ground rules are a helpful starting place for the RE teacher dealing with the thorny issues surrounding freedom of speech in the classroom. Many of these rules will be embedded in the excellent practice of thousands of RE teachers who, perhaps rightly, view themselves as experts in their own school settings when it comes to managing difficult dialogue or issues in class. If we read closely enough, perhaps Jackson also helps the RE teacher deal with the confusion, previously highlighted, with the British government's definition of 'fundamental British values' (FBV). The FBV agenda maintains that pupils should 'develop mutual respect and tolerance of different faiths and beliefs' (Home Office 2011, p.107). As discussed above, this definition is so philosophically vague that it would for instance 'force' a student critical of infant circumcision to show respect and tolerance for a view they find abhorrent. Likewise, a student who is alive thanks to a blood transfusion would be 'forced' to show respect and tolerance to a Jehovah's Witness student who would rather die than receive someone else's blood. These may appear extreme examples, but I offer them to highlight the logical contradictions found within the FBV agenda. Values are claims to truth and are therefore universal. To claim them as being specific to a nation state is, like an astronaut planting a flag on the moon, sheer idiocy.

Jackson's rules offer us a slightly better framework for dealing with unsafe issues in the RE classroom. Note that he argues: 'Respect should be shown for the right of others to express views and beliefs different from one's own' (2014, p.56). This is clearer in that it does not, as the FBV agenda seems to imply, argue that education should foster mutual respect and tolerance for different beliefs without defining why mutual respect and tolerance for all beliefs is an inherent good. It instead maintains the principle, oft (mis)attributed to Voltaire, that 'I may disagree with what you say but I will defend to the death your right to say it.' Jackson also, helpfully, highlights that (and this is the thing students and teachers sometimes find tricky) when discussing controversial issues, it is the ideas that people express that should be challenged, not the individuals who express them. Far too often students take a criticism of the ideas they are expressing as a personal slight or an *ad hominem* attack. I have seen RE teachers do the same when others have criticised their ideas online and in social media forums. If RE teachers can do anything well, it must be to help our students learn not that all answers are good/right answers and that when we criticise we do not 'play the man' but instead we always 'play the ball'. This will not always be easy. As Jackson himself admits in the conclusion to his chapter, 'All classroom interaction involves some degree of risk, especially when controversial issues are discussed and different claims to truth are made' (2014, p.57).

Classroom tools for managing 'unsafe' topics

We might end by concluding that there are two distinct approaches to dealing with unsafe ideas in the RE classroom: debate and dialogue. Debate adopts a dialectical approach, whereby an idea is put forward that is then robustly contested. In the Socratic sense, it is confrontational and argumentative. It forces students to see logical contradictions in arguments or positions that they or others are defending. An alternative approach centred on dialogue aims to foster mutual understanding through 'safe' encounters with those whose beliefs, culture or views might be alien, or opposed, to one's own.

Formal debate

Most students' experience of parliamentary debating will be watching the weekly bear-pit politics of Prime Minister's Questions. It is certainly an unedifying introduction into the formalities of academic debate. The English-Speaking Union provide some excellent free resources for schools new to debating, and you will be able to see examples on their Vimeo and YouTube channels. Debate is a classroom tool that requires students to adopt intellectual positions that are not necessarily ones they agree with and to consider arguments and points of view they might find offensive. For example, when wanting to teach the issues surrounding the Charlie Hebdo attacks one could construct a motion 'This House supports the publication of cartoons of Muhammad'. For many students, this is a controversial and even inflammatory statement. But in a liberal democracy it is a statement that should be discussed. Formal debating provides students with a safe space in which to argue and to know that (under Jackson's rules) they are challenging the ideas, not the individuals expressing them. Specific details on how formal debating can be used as a tool to discuss unsafe ideas in RE can be found in my 2012 Farmington Fellowship Report (McKain 2012).

Dialogue

Interfaith dialogue should be a vital component of any successful RE curriculum. Many schools run a variety of interfaith activities (visitors, conferences, etc.) that give students an opportunity to converse with speakers and representatives from a diverse group of faiths and religions. Whilst this might be easier for some schools, such as those in a multi-faith or multi-ethnic location or with a diverse intake, schools in more homogeneous settings can use technology to help embed interfaith understanding. The education charity Generation Global is run by the Tony Blair Faith Foundation and offers students the opportunity to communicate with students from over twenty countries across the world through videoconferences and online dialogue. They maintain that dialogue needs to be understood as a separate form of communication from debating. In formal debating the rules say that the person who has the best argument is the winner. In dialogue the process is reciprocal and each participant learns from the other. They may not choose to agree but they, acknowledging difference over controversial issues, might bridge a hitherto-unbridgeable gap between two opposing parties. A teacher who has used the programme writes:

> The real benefit of the programme is the opportunity to interact with pupils in different cultures across the globe... The video conference in particular brought huge benefits to my pupils, helping them to broaden their understanding of the significance and complexities of faith and citizenship issues in another culture. (Generation Global 2016)

Conclusion

I began this chapter with a quotation from a philosopher who more than any other has defined arguments over freedom of speech. It would be impossible to write a chapter on freedom of speech and not include him. John Stuart Mill realised that where freedom of speech was curtailed, freedom of thought would not be possible. However, in *On Liberty*, Mill (1859/1974) clearly advocates paternalism when dealing with children and those unable to apply sufficient reason. Freedom is good, argues Mill, for it will ultimately promote utility. In defence of that good, one must always be prepared to be proved wrong. Integral to education is that it provides students with the knowledge, skills and character to adopt an idea and then defend it. Therefore, a safe space to discuss unsafe ideas cannot take place in a relativist, postmodern vacuum where all answers are right and no opinions are wrong. In the RE classroom, and in other classrooms, a safe space is seen as part of the history of the Academy where ideas can be robustly debated and where differences in opinion can be shared and challenged.

References

Dawkins, R. (2014) 'Are there emotional no-go areas where logic dare not show its face?' [Blog post]. Richard Dawkins Foundation. Accessed on 30 May 2017 at https://richarddawkins.net/2014/07/are-there-emotional-no-go-areas-where-logic-dare-not-show-its-face

Department for Education (2015) *The Prevent Duty: Departmental Advice for Schools and Childcare Providers*. London: DfE. Accessed on 30 May 2017 at http://dera.ioe.ac.uk/23408/1/prevent-duty-departmental-advice-v6.pdf

Dinham, A. and Shaw, M. (2015) *RE for REal: The Future of Teaching and Learning about Religion and Belief*. Accessed on 29 May 2017 via http://research.gold.ac.uk/19628

Fox, C. (2016) *I Find that Offensive*. London: Biteback.

Generation Global (2016) 'How the program runs in your country: United Kingdom.' Accessed on 25 June 2017 at https://generation.global

Harris, R. (2009) 'Freedom of speech and philosophy of education.' *British Journal of Educational Studies 57*, 2, 111–126.

Hillman, N. (2016) *Keeping Schtum: What Students Think of Free Speech*. Oxford: Higher Education Policy Unit. Accessed 30 May 2017 at www.hepi.ac.uk/wp-content/uploads/2016/05/Hepi_Keeping-Schtum-Report-85-Web.pdf

Home Office (2011) *Prevent Strategy*. Cm 8092. Accessed 25 June 2017 at www.gov.uk/government/uploads/system/uploads/attachment_data/file/97976/prevent-strategy-review.pdf

Jackson, R. (2014) *Signposts: Policy and Practice for Teaching about Religions and Non-religious Worldviews in Intercultural Education*. Strasbourg: Council of Europe Publishing.

Jones, O. (2015, 1 July) 'Government policy will seal the mouths of Muslim pupils.' *The Guardian*. Accessed on 30 May 2017 at www.theguardian.com/commentisfree/2015/jul/01/muslim-children-enemy-radicalisation

Lewis, A. (2015, 8 July) 'RE: Radicalism and extremism' [Blog post]. TDRE Boss. Accessed on 30 May 2017 at http://tdreboss.blogspot.co.uk/2015/07/re-radicalism-and-extremism.html

McKain, N. (2012) *'Order... Order' – Why RS is the Best Subject in School for Encouraging Formal Debating*. Farmington Fellowship Report TT288. Accessed at hwww.farmington.ac.uk/index.php/tt288-order-order-why-rs-is-the-best-subject-in-school-for-encouraging-formal-debating

Mill, J.S. (1974) *On Liberty*. London: Penguin. (Original work published 1859.)

Prime Minister's Office (2015, 17 September) 'PM's Extremism Taskforce: Tackling extremism in universities and colleges top of the agenda' [Press release]. Accessed on 30 May 2017 at www.gov.uk/government/news/pms-extremism-taskforce-tackling-extremism-in-universities-and-colleges-top-of-the-agenda

Welby, J. (2016, 9 November) 'I'm an extremist, according to the Govt's definition.' The Christian Institute. Accessed on 30 May 2017 at www.christian.org.uk/news/justin-welby-im-extremist-according-govts-definition

Chapter 12

THE ROLE OF RELIGIOUS EDUCATION IN ADDRESSING EXTREMISM

ADAM WHITLOCK

Questions are sometimes asked about the place and relevance of contemporary religious education in the school curriculum because of students' experiences of religion as portrayed in the media and the links made between religion and violence, hate and fundamentalism at global and national levels, and for many students, at the local level of their daily lives. This chapter presents an underlying philosophy and pedagogy of religious education shaped by specific case studies linked with violence, hate, fundamentalism and the British government's Prevent strategy.

Introduction: Contemporary threats

The world our students live in is one in which violent acts of terror have dominated the political, social, economic and, more importantly, the religious landscape. If ever there was a need to ask the common question in a religious education curriculum, 'How far does religion cause conflict?', it is now. The classroom has become the place for discussion about extreme acts of violence and the vitriol from radical preachers. It might have been the case that in RE lessons much of what has been discussed, since 9/11, has been drawn from global media; however, in recent years, since the July 2005 bombings in

London, it has become more common, in English RE classrooms, to find students discussing what they have seen and heard in their local community. The influence of extreme views upon young people, whether they be political or religious, is evident in our society, and a duty has been laid upon schools to tackle these alien ideologies that breach 'fundamental British values'.

Already there will be several issues raised by what some might refer to as the above rhetoric: 'What do you mean by extremism and fundamentalism?', 'Isn't this creating an unnecessary fear in society?', 'Is it right to impose upon schools a duty to report radicalisation?' and 'What exactly are fundamental British values?' I cannot address these questions and do them justice here, therefore I have assumed the acceptance of the statutory duty imposed upon schools by the British government and that there is a common understanding of what radical extremism is, outlined by the Home Office (2015):

> Extremism is the vocal or active opposition to our fundamental values, including democracy, the rule of law, individual liberty and the mutual respect and tolerance of different faiths and beliefs. We also regard calls for the death of members of our armed forces as extremist. (p.9)

With Brexit and the recent US election, the divided society our students live in has become more apparent, often polarised by identity politics and hate speech. It is my belief that religious education can equip students with the tools necessary to discern the possible threats that surround them and to process extreme narratives in a critical way. I am suggesting three areas that, in my experience, are helpful in enabling religious education to deal with these issues.

Challenging threats through religious literacy

Teachers need to design an effective religious education curriculum that generates religiously literate students who can identify views and examine them critically. This argument suggests that a basic understanding of literacy is not enough. Most schools have a teacher who is responsible for students' literacy, and in some schools there are literacy representatives from every subject who meet regularly, as a team, to shape and implement school policy in this area. However, I believe, it is not enough for our students to know how to engage with polemical texts and ideologies. A religiously literate student is one who can access the skill of critical understanding and apply it to extreme narratives with caution. This goes beyond the basic literacy all students receive. Lynn Davies (2009, p.185) puts it succinctly: 'We want young people to be idealistic and to challenge injustice where they see it; but the task is to politicise young people without cementing uncritical acceptance of single truths.' If we create religiously literate students, then we can safely 'politicise' them by sharing the variations in worldview and allow them to engage in critical reflection.

It would be right to identify what a religiously literate student looks like. Diane L. Moore (2006) from Harvard Divinity School has proposed the following:

> Religious literacy entails the ability to discern and analyse the fundamental intersections of religion and social/political/cultural life through multiple lenses. Specifically, a religiously literate person will possess 1) a basic understanding of the history, central texts (where applicable), beliefs, practices and contemporary manifestations of several of the world's religious traditions as they arose out of and continue to be shaped by particular social, historical and cultural contexts; and 2) the ability to discern and explore the religious dimensions of political, social and cultural expressions across time and place. (p.3)

The emphasis on 'discern' and 'analyse' are key features of religious literacy and play a fundamental role in generating a healthy balanced student. Quite often the polemical rhetoric of radicalised individuals is void of contextual understanding and analysis of varying dimensions that make up a religious belief.

It is important that our students develop these skills so they can engage with the world outside the classroom from a rational and balanced perspective. These skills can safeguard their interests within the realist assumption that they will be exposed to extreme narratives whether we protect them in school or not. As Ed Pawson, then chairman of the National Association of Teachers of Religious Education, stated at 'Strictly RE' (its first national conference) in 2015: 'The development of religious literacy in young people in the UK could help to make them less vulnerable to religious radicalisation' (Burns, 2015).

I would wish to take this further and propose that staff who are not religious educators need to develop some level of basic religious literacy to engage with students in their classrooms about issues that arise in their subject area. For example, one time I had a student referred to me because of his response to a discussion on the Charlie Hebdo murders. 'I think it's right they got killed – they drew an image of the Prophet' was his contribution. Concerned why he would say such a thing, the teacher asked me to have a conversation to establish whether he was serious and if this should become a Prevent issue. I believe the teacher took the right course of action in referring the student so that I could establish grounds for his comments. Building a quick rapport with the student was key in receiving a genuine open response. Having previously taught the student, this was an easy task. Once I asked about his comments, he at first did not understand why it was an issue. The moment I asked him some theologically challenging questions it all became apparent. The dialogue went something like this:

Teacher: So, tell me about the comments you recently made about the Charlie Hebdo attacks.

Student: Ah, I was just saying how these guys that drew the Prophet got what they deserved.

Teacher: That's an interesting view. Tell me, does it say anywhere in the Quran that if you draw an image of the Prophet Muhammad you should be executed?

Student: I'm not sure.

Teacher: I'll help you out. It doesn't.

Student: Oh, I didn't know that.

Teacher: Out of interest, what would your parents say about your views?

Student: Thinking about it, I reckon they would disagree with me.

Teacher: Why is that?

Student: Because they don't condone violence.

[*At this moment, his face drops with the realisation that his words were immature and ill-thought.*]

Teacher: Can you see how you said something without thinking it through properly and have given the wrong impression of Islam to a non-Muslim?

Student: Oh, I'm sorry, I didn't think about it like that.

Teacher: Don't be sorry, just be aware that you should think about what you believe and why you believe it. Sometimes it ends up sounding different to how we feel.

Student: Thanks, Sir.

This conversation showed me at the time that students will often say provocative things without much forethought. I am pleased this boy did speak his mind and that the teacher felt comfortable referring him. I thoroughly enjoyed helping him see for himself that he had no basis for adhering to his statement, but I was only able to do this and challenge his outburst with a religiously literate dialogue about the Quran and Islamic belief. It is plausible to assume that if the teacher had some basic understanding of Islam that they could have had a similar short conversation with the boy after the lesson and then write up the situation for safeguarding records.

These records are internal for the school to keep, to grasp the wider picture should other similar instances arise and to track the way in which the situation was handled, which does not have a negative impact on the student's future. The only time these records would be shared are when there is a need to safeguard the student and others by working with external agencies, such as the social services or police. There is a basis here for religious education specialists to capitalise on the opportunity of whole-school training annually to new staff in basic religious literacy that is contextualised within the issues surrounding the school. This would empower staff with a general religious literacy, as the teacher who referred the student seemed to have when identifying the concern.

Challenging threats through a triad of studies

Historically, English religious education was the study of God and moral living within Christianity, generally known as confessional religious education. The Christian narrative was learnt through the study of the Bible and doctrine was taught as truth. With the introduction of phenomenological religious education, influenced by Ninian Smart (1968), religious education moved away from dogma as the religious aspect of lessons took the shape of 'objectivity and empathy'. With the influence of Smart's (1989) dimensions of religion, many religious education curricula focused on the application of ethical and social dimensions of religion to contemporary issues in the modern world. Thus, the sociological aspect of religion was emphasised, sometimes at the cost of theological depth. This can be seen in previous specifications for the General Certificate of Secondary Education (GCSE) with textbooks that reflect a thematic and social approach such as the Edexcel (2012) specification. It has been suggested by Barnes (2006) that:

> British religious education has misrepresented the nature of religion in efforts to commend itself as contributing to the

social aims of education, as these are typically framed in liberal democratic societies such as Britain in terms of furthering tolerance, respect for difference and social cohesion. (p.396)

He points out that this is ironic as the very agenda this shift in religious education sought to address has been superficially dealt with to the detriment of its social aims and the general reputation of the subject. Furthermore, Britain has also shifted in attitude towards religion with the rise of secularisation and postmodern attitudes to spirituality. Students were becoming dissatisfied with learning about religion and wanted their curiosity inspired and the subject to be attractive, especially if they were to pursue it to Advanced Level.

As a result of this shift, many schools simply made a name change from Religious Education to Philosophy and Ethics. This shift in name created a vacuum in theological depth and students were left with a social curriculum that touched upon aspects of religion, and questioned religion, but rarely engaged with sacred texts and truth claims. With the recent exam reform by the Office of Qualifications and Examinations Regulation (Ofqual), religious education seems to have a balanced study of religion, philosophy and ethics.

It could be argued that this triad of theology, philosophy and sociology in a curriculum has addressed one of the flaws in the teaching of religious education. Therefore, with this new trinity of equilibrium, religious education is positioned well to tackle the contemporary threat from violent and non-violent extremism, fundamentalism, identity politics and hate speech. Put in simplistic terms, with good religious literacy, students can access the sociology of religion and understand the many contexts from which religious truth claims emerge. They can undertake the philosophical enquiry necessary to challenge truth claims and critically evaluate arguments that are given from a variety of worldviews. They can access the theological depth necessary to engage with the hermeneutics of scripture and recognise the multiple-lens that is required to be exegetical instead of eisegetical when reading texts. These skills are essential to cultivate a competent student, ready to deal with the ever-transient globalised world.

Challenging threats through critical realism

I was fortunate enough to train at King's College London for my Postgraduate Certificate of Education and then complete a Master's in Religious Education under Professor Andrew Wright. It was around this time in 2007 that Wright had integrated Roy Bhaskar's philosophical approach of critical realism and applied it as a pedagogy in religious education. I was also able to get involved in the Forum for Religious and Spiritual Education group of writers and put into practice the pedagogical model that was being discussed, now known as Critical Religious Education. This model of religious education is a reaction to the pluralist and secular postmodern worldview by proposing that there should be a pursuit of ultimate truth in the classroom that should not be avoided. Wright (2007) underpins his approach with a critical-realist philosophy that is based on the concepts of ontological realism, epistemic relativism and judgemental rationality.

In my own faculty, I interpret these as expression, exploration and evaluation. These three objectives set the tone for every lesson in my curriculum. Whilst I am aware this is only one pedagogy to draw from, I noticed that the opportunity for students to express their ontological reality was also an occasion for any fundamental truth claim to be aired in a lesson. Furthermore, offering students a variety of challenging and often controversial worldviews to explore gave them the opportunity to be challenged themselves as they learn. Finally, the opening given to students by the end of a lesson or a scheme of work, to make rational judgements and evaluate the stimulus explored, meant they either changed from extreme and intolerant to moderate and tolerant views, or at the very least, had a better understanding of why they believed what they believed: a far less dangerous claim than having absolute truth with no openness to challenge.

One time, I invited a group of Year 11 Muslim boys and girls to engage with a pilot course commissioned by the Psychology Department at Cambridge University. It is called 'Being Muslim, Being British'. This short course (IC Thinking 2016) aims to expose students to extreme narratives and develop their integrative complexity. The argument is that:

> Low complexity reasoning often leads to conflict (even violent conflict) because nuanced collaborative solutions are, by definition, screened out as the black and white, intransigent demands of one group are pitted against the black and white demands of the other. Dogmatic authoritarianism, the inability to engage in trade-offs, and low integrative complexity all seem to be undergirded by similar cognitive processes in which either *freezing* or *seizing* on to certain outcomes makes thinking rigid. (Liht and Savage 2013, p.46)

I have often heard teachers deny students the opportunity to discuss the contemporary threats that exist on their doorstep for fear that they will enter unknown territory and entertain politically incorrect rhetoric. However, opening the channels to communication in the classroom is the safest place for this 'extreme dialogue' and allows students to challenge rigid ideology.

Recently I have discovered a series of short powerful videos that facilitate 'extreme dialogue' by the think-tank Institute for Strategic Dialogue. These short, free, easy-to-access videos[1] take students through the extreme narratives of once radicalised people from a variety of backgrounds, including the Northern Ireland conflict, Islamic extremism and racial hate speech. These are the kinds of stimuli that can challenge students' worldviews and introduce them to truth claims for rational evaluation. I have found that students enjoy engaging with these debates and

---

[1]   http://extremedialogue.org/#stories

can identify for themselves what is considered acceptable and unacceptable ideologies. Therefore, it is important to embed the aforementioned fundamental British values in a curriculum like religious education in order to empower students with the knowledge to identify what is acceptable and unacceptable.

Prevent – a case study

With the statutory duty introduced by the Department for Education (2015) that all schools in England must refer any student to their local Prevent team when concerned about radicalisation, it became necessary for schools to implement a Prevent policy as part of their safeguarding procedures. In my school, I helped shape the policy to ensure we had a clear understanding of what to do when concerns are raised over a student, rather than some arbitrary document shaped by anecdote. I had some experiences in mind that influenced the way in which we would approach this issue. I want to share a case study of how we came to address the contemporary threats, in their complex manifestations, at our door.

Some years ago, I taught a student who was going through the start of an identity crisis. This is not an uncommon find as a teacher in a secondary school, but it was the ideology that came with this new-found identity that was concerning. The student's parents were also concerned and initially raised the alarm by meeting the Principal to share their anxieties. The student was a Muslim from a minority group and had been mentored and influenced by an Imam, residing in England, who was a fugitive from the Middle East. This Imam was known to the police for extreme views towards other Muslim groups. The concern was never that this student would be a harm to others, but more a harm to himself by being in the centre of hostility. It was the trust the Principal placed in me to speak with the student that began a series of meetings that would shape how my school dealt with these scenarios for the future. At the time, nothing was in place to deal with radicalisation.

Scroll back a few years before this and there was a different student, who just before completing sixth form, was heavily influenced by a brother who had become a foreign fighter in Syria for Daesh. This student sat away from others when an outside speaker was addressing the class about their Christian faith. The student's behaviour was strange, as they stood up and spoke in Arabic before addressing the speaker with a challenging question about their beliefs. It was not until after this student left the school that we realised the full extent of the issues they were struggling with, reconciling their faith in Islam with fighting for a twisted cause. The police were already involved in this student's life because of the brother's actions and this seemed to cause further alienation from Western society. After this extremely able student left school they unfortunately wound up in Syria fighting for Daesh and were killed in combat. This student's life will leave an indelible print on my mind, forever serving to strengthen my resolve in creating a safe environment in schools to tackle extreme narratives that warp our young people into false and malevolent worldviews.

Therefore, when this further student was a concern, I wanted to cultivate a relationship that went beyond the role of teacher and entered the domain of mentor. Fortunately, having taught this student and built up a good relationship to begin with, this was an easy prospect to orchestrate. The student was enthusiastic about speaking to me outside lesson time regarding religious and political issues in contemporary media, and developed a fascination with various news outlets which fuelled a worldview and strengthened a discrimination against another Muslim group. The external mentor who was fuelling this discrimination was an international fugitive who was appearing on web-based TV networks, which the student would access from home regularly, listening to his mantra. Occasionally the student would kiss the screen to show respect and allegiance as a follower. Whilst it seemed that the student's ideologies were concrete, their identity seemed pliable. I knew it would take time but relationship was the key. I organised regular informal meetings to catch up on academic work and discuss the news. It did not take long for the student to become open about views on Islam and the West. In a well-read, intellectual manner, the student cited source after source to back up the rhetoric. Most of the time these views were just semi-controversial, which is not anything unusual in a religious education lesson; however, when veneration of the mentor played a part in the foundation of the argument and hate speech occurred, this is when it became important to intervene. The religious education the student received ran alongside these conversations, and being equipped with a critical-realist approach to religion seemed to open the student's mind just enough for useful dialogue. Spending a considerable time listening to the student's worldview built trust between us, and naturally the relationship grew into one of mentor and mentee. This was vital for any challenge to any worldview to be effective. There was a high level of religious literacy necessary to engage with this student, which other members of staff were unable to utilise. It was at this point I realised that subject specialists in religious education can draw from a set of skills that others cannot, even those in senior posts such as the lead teacher for child protection. Once I had established a clear focus for discussion, I was able to bring the student around to the point of referral and set up a meeting with the local Prevent team.

At first this whole process was daunting, having heard the stories from other schools that had poor experiences of Prevent in the past owing to a heavy handed approach. I have to admit that I was reticent in dealing with these 'strangers' and introducing them to one of my students. There was absolutely no way this was going to work unless the student had trust in the relationship I had built so carefully. The first meeting was set up and the student spent the first 20 minutes lying about their beliefs. Once I could convince the student that these men were safe to talk to, the conversation began to cover contacts and influences. An intervention provider who was also a Muslim was assigned to the student. l arranged the meetings and ensured that the student was comfortable with the process whilst the parents were aware of the arrangements and showed support. Over a period of six months, these meetings took place and l attended the Channel Panel discussions to establish the progress that was made. At every point, l was consulted by the team as to what the best course of action was and l am very grateful for the collaborative process that took place. l am aware that not every Prevent team demonstrates such sensitivity, and this is a wider issue that needs to be addressed by the Home Office to ensure schools can be comfortable in referring students under this new statutory duty.

The result of this process was that the student was guided gently to freely realise that the held views were not conducive to achieving the type of society the student wanted to be part of. Any future ambitions to work as a civil servant would have been nullified by such attitudes and any attendant conduct, which in turn helped the student realise the limitations that would come from such a worldview. Furthermore, the religious ideologies professed were challenged by a version of Islam being presented by trusted subject specialists. l suspect that if you were to ask this student today, as a mature adult in civilised society, why they changed their mind, the answer would be 'because of respect and relationship', meaning the connection formed with people who identified intolerant views but gave the time of day to share them and were not afraid to challenge any arguments that make up the fundamental British values of our society.

l believe there are many other students who need to be reached through religious literacy: a challenging pedagogy in the classroom that can bring intolerant ideologies to the surface with a curriculum that is not afraid to tackle 'truth claims'.

The role of religious education

During a time of questions and answers at a conference l was speaking at, one RE teacher opened with the declaration:

'I'm disappointed in this keynote speech today, as the argument put forward seems to suggest that the role of RE is to tackle radicalisation and extremism, and I couldn't disagree more.' It must be clear that I do not believe tackling radicalisation is the main role of religious education in any school. The subject transcends all political policy and has far greater roles than this. However, I am certain that in the current climate, RE is well positioned to deal with extreme narratives that our students might encounter.

With fundamental British values high on the agenda of our government, this could be an opportunity for RE to raise its profile in schools as the forerunner for training staff to become religiously literate and embedding an emphasis on religious literacy within the curriculum. Furthermore, a curriculum that embraces the new exam reform and ensures all year groups have a healthy dose of the triad of theology, sociology and philosophy can only serve to offer our students breadth and depth in studies that will equip them with hermeneutics, context and judgemental rationality. There are many pedagogies at our disposal, but it is clear to me that Critical Religious Education is well equipped to challenge harmful truth claims. In the same way that my former students' lives serve as a reminder to me of the reality we face in education today, avoiding the difficult calling that has evolved for RE teachers facing contemporary threats of violent and non-violent extremism, fundamentalism, identity politics and hate speech is not an option. Holding on to truth claims is important, but allowing students to hold on to extreme ideologies that are harmful to them and society without any intervention is inexcusable.

References

Barnes, P. (2006) 'The misrepresentation of religion in modern British (religious) education.' *British Journal of Educational Studies* 54, 4, 396–412.

Burns, J. (2015) 'Religious education classes "needed" in schools.' BBC News. Accessed on 25 June 2017 at www.bbc.co.uk/news/education-30989933

Davies, L. (2009) 'Educating against extremism: Towards a critical politicisation of young people'. *International Review of Education* 55, 2/3, 185–201.

Department for Education (2015) *The Prevent Duty: Departmental Advice for Schools and Childcare Providers*. London: DfE. Accessed on 30 May 2017 at http://dera.ioe.ac.uk/23408/1/prevent-duty-departmental-advice-v6.pdf

Edexcel (2012) *Specification Edexcel GCSE in Religious Studies for First Certification 2013 Issue 5*. Accessed on 25 June 2017 at http://qualifications.pearson.com/content/dam/pdf/GCSE/ReligiousStudies/2009/Specificationandsample assessments/GCSE_Religious_Studies_Spec_2012.pdf

Home Office (2015) *Counter-Extremism Strategy*, Cm 9148. London: The Stationery Office.

IC Thinking *Being Muslim, Being British*. Accessed on 29 October 2016 at https://sites.google.com/site/icthinking/being-muslim-being-british

Liht, J. and Savage, S. (2013) 'Preventing violent extremism through value complexity: Being Muslim being British.' *Journal of Strategic Security* 6, 4, 46–61.

Moore, D.L. (2006) 'Overcoming religious illiteracy: A cultural studies approach.' *World History Connected* 4, 1, 3–8.

Smart, N. (1968) *Secular Education and the Logic of Religion*. London: Faber and Faber.

Smart, N. (1989) *The World's Religions*. Cambridge: Cambridge University Press.

Wright, A. (2007) *Critical Religious Education, Multiculturalism and the Pursuit of Truth*. Cardiff: University of Wales Press.

Chapter 13

FAITH COMMUNITIES AS STAKEHOLDERS IN RELIGIOUS EDUCATION

A Commitment to Generous Hospitality

DEREK HOLLOWAY

The involvement of faith communities in religious education (RE) has always been contentious, but I wish to argue that by and large such involvement has been positive and has become an established part of the subject's educational landscape. In this chapter I will propose that this is in significant part due to an approach I call 'generous hospitality', which, I believe, has been the hallmark of the faith communities. It is a term taken from a recent Church of England publication but does, I feel, capture the working relationship that I have observed first as a Head of RE in a community school and as a member of a Standing Advisory Council on Religious Education and its working parties, then as a diocesan and, later, a local education authority adviser leading syllabus reviews, and latterly working nationally for the Church of England Education Office. I will argue that generous hospitality is not just about the time, money and resources that faith communities have devoted to RE – for that there could be mixed motives – but it is a commitment to want to seek the best RE for all pupils in all schools. It is an investment in an increasing professionalism toward the subject, a willingness to 'step up' when there is need, and to seek and find solutions to the issues the subject has faced. It is a hospitality that welcomes and works with those of all faiths and none, not out of an interfaith nicety but out of a spirit of genuine respect for difference. It is a hospitality that will listen and willingly take on the latest advice and thinking and is not stuck in old orthodoxies. Furthermore, I will suggest that this spirit of generous hospitality is now crucial in taking the subject forward in a time of impending systems change to a more national rather than locally based provision. Much of what follows is personal reflection and observation from a 30-year journey in the centre of this contention.

Introduction

Faith community engagement is one of the distinctive features of the English and Welsh system of RE. Faith communities have a deep and reasonable desire to ensure that their beliefs and practices are accurately and fairly reflected in the classroom. Their motives for this will run the gamut from a desire to support pupils of the faith community in their personal faith development while at school, to a broader concern for what is currently called 'social cohesion'. All faith communities, including the secular and humanist groups, will, of course, welcome greater interest in their beliefs. They may be less keen on a critical analysis of these beliefs and attendant practices. This is where it becomes contentious and potentially problematic for academic study. When does a reasonable desire to show a faith in a positive light become proselytising? When, if at all, does the need to support the spiritual growth of a young believer trump a look at the more negative aspects of religious practice? When does the requirement to promote the government's fundamental British value of mutual respect and tolerance of those of different faiths and beliefs militate against a critical evaluation of religious teaching? The tension lies around who defines what is 'accurate' and what is 'fair'. This is what I heard Lynn Revell of Canterbury Christ Church University describe recently in a debate at the 'Battle of Ideas' conference in 2016. As the 'cultural capital' of RE, her argument was that this definition should lie with the professional RE community, not the faith community. The tension is perhaps at its greatest when the provision of RE is undergoing a systems change, as in 1988 and, arguably, still today.

Generous hospitality

For the most part, this tension has been well managed, and faith community involvement is recognised and valued by the wider RE community as at first Christianity, then other world faiths, and latterly non-religious worldviews have given their time and capacity to making RE the best it can be. I would like to categorise this engagement by the faith communities as a form of 'generous hospitality': generous in resources and time, and hospitable in wanting to work with others. In the recently published Church of England Education Office's *Vision for Education* (2016b), it was put this way:

> Such an approach is offered through a commitment to generous hospitality, being true to our underpinning faith but with a deep respect for the integrity of other traditions and beliefs, and for the religious freedom of each person. (p.13)

It is this commitment to that 'generous hospitality' that drives the work of the Church of England in RE. It is a generous hospitality that extends to all pupils in all schools as all pupils are seen as growing up in a diocese. This contrasts with an approach that might have been concerned only with pupils growing up in the faith community or attending faith community schools, as may be found in other countries. I would contend that the Church of England began this approach, which others have enthusiastically followed.

For the Church of England this approach goes back to Joshua Watson who founded the National Society (now known as the Church of England Education Office) in 1811. John Gay (2016) recently described the National Society as 'the initiator of mass schooling in the 19th century' (p.303). One of the aims of the organisation was 'promoting religious instruction', and although Joshua Watson might not recognise some of what we now call 'religious education' taught in church schools today, the commitment to promoting the subject remains at the heart of the vision of church schools. Promoting RE is not only in the trust deed, it is in the DNA of church schools.

A new dispensation

Religious education, as we know it in schools today, really dates from the 1988 Education Act (Education Reform Act 1988, Section 8(3), repeated in the Education Act 1996 Section 375(3) and the School Standards and Framework Act 1998 Schedule 19(5), and subsequent Acts). There is much that can be written about the context and impact of this Act. Here I will highlight just two points that I feel are significant in the context of this chapter.

- For the first time, national government insisted that religious education, as it was now legally designated, should have broad content. The Act stated, specifically, that religious education 'shall reflect the fact that religious traditions are in the main Christian whilst taking into account the teachings and practice of the other principal religions in Great Britain' (Section 8). There are problems with this wording, but what is clear is two-fold: religious education syllabuses were to be 'in the main' Christian, but other principal religions were also to be taught. Along with these changes, within the composition of each local education authority's Standing Advisory Council on Religious Education (SACRE), religious traditions other than Christianity were now to sit alongside Christianity in syllabus construction.

- The 1988 Act brought in the National Curriculum, and while RE was not to be a National Curriculum subject, it now had to justify itself on educational grounds alongside all other curriculum subjects. RE did not have to have attainment targets, programmes of study or assessment, but these could be recommended...and recommended they were!

A SACRE now needed the guidance of a professional adviser, who was not only an expert in a range of traditions, but also fluent in the language of educational pedagogy and methodology. The result was a creative time for RE, and this new breed of adviser had the latest research, ideas and approaches at their fingertips. Many, recruited direct from the classroom, carried with them an authority based on that professional expertise. They took their place alongside the subject advisers now supporting schools for the National Curriculum subjects, but additionally they had the chance to create new, local curricula rather than help schools to implement a centrally set curriculum. They remade RE as we know it today.

As each of the (currently) 153 SACREs across the country set up their working parties of teachers to draft their folders full of syllabuses, curriculum guidance, suggested schemes of work, policies and moderated work, the wheel was re-invented many times up and down the country. The requirement to review the Agreed Syllabus every five years gave this process a self-perpetuating momentum. The Church of England and other faith community representatives were invited to these working parties, but as most were experts in their faith rather than RE professionals, they were soon lost in the new educational jargon of classroom practice. They checked the accuracy of the terminology but contributed little to the structure. The cultural capital of the subject was shifting into the hands of the subject 'professionals'. Many faith representatives felt marginalised. Their support was needed to get the syllabus passed, but their contributions were often questioned as confessional and not educationally sound.

Faith community response

At this point the faith communities could have retired gracefully into the background, accepting that they were no longer needed now the 'experts' were here. For the Church of England, a commitment to RE was at the core of what church schools were set up to provide, which meant it would remain involved in RE. The dioceses began to employ their own religious education advisers with a teaching and professional background on SACREs to replace their less professional representatives, who were often clergy. These advisers were more likely to be drawn from the primary classroom than the secondary, and they were more likely to be women. All took a greater interest in collective worship than their local authority colleagues. They were likely to be part-funded by Anglican church college trusts and often they had a dual role involving them with support for children and youth work. (For more on the generous hospitality of the Church college trusts see John Gay (2016, Chapter 12).) These factors combined to limit their influence on SACREs and on syllabuses and classroom RE. They did, however, bring with them the same ideas, approaches and training as local education authority RE advisers. This was the beginning of the professionalisation of faith community advisers. These advisers would increasingly hold their own, but at first they were very much the junior partners producing additional guidance for church schools alone.

This guidance often took the form of additional ideas for teaching aspects of Christianity in church schools. Spurred on by the demands of denominational inspection, this became known as 'additionality'. For the most part these resources sought to complement the locally Agreed Syllabus, but the growing variation of approach of Agreed Syllabuses and lack of coherence between local authority and diocesan boundaries made this increasingly problematic. For example, in the 1990s Winchester and Salisbury dioceses collaborated on a resource that attempted to bridge a gap between two increasingly divergent county syllabuses in Hampshire and Dorset. Resources like

Festival Matters (Holloway *et al.* 2014) that replaced it across the Salisbury diocese and much of the south-west, focused on the progressive and systematic study of aspects of Christianity such as festivals or core concepts such as the Trinity. These resources were often made available to community schools free or at very little more than printing cost. This was an approach that would re-surface more recently. However, these were occasional complementary resources; most of the curriculum, even in church schools, was delivered in line with the local syllabus using the same classroom practice encouraged by the local authority.

Equally, nor were the other faith communities, newly empowered, prepared to sit back for long. A general concern about being misrepresented in the media meant that many faith communities felt the need to become engaged with RE. Across the country, representatives from Jewish, Muslim and other faith backgrounds came forward to offer workshops in schools to support these new syllabuses. For example, Tariq Palmer of the Bournemouth Islamic Centre became a regular visitor to schools across Dorset, tirelessly and generously giving of his time and travel free to help pupils understand more about Islam. His work was mirrored across the country. Members of the faith communities took days off work to ensure places of worship were opened for school visits. Leaflets and artefacts box projects were produced to provide teachers with some background knowledge to help them teach accurately about the community under study. The Muslim Council of Britain's artefacts box project was a national version of many local initiatives.

Recent years have seen the British Humanist Association (BHA) become more active in the RE world. They followed the faith community lead, producing resources to explain Humanist ideas with the offer of speakers from the community to come and talk in schools. Perhaps because they are later entrants, or perhaps because of the nature of Humanism, they have sought to provide resources on a national basis rather than locally. Slowly this engagement with the curriculum content of RE, this generous hospitality, spread. The decision by the BHA to engage more actively in supporting RE was a significant milestone. The decision taken to resource and support RE at a national level through website resources rather than through local resourcing of the Agreed Syllabus was the shape of things to come.

From the mid-'noughties' onwards local authority budgets became increasingly squeezed. Early casualties were many of the subject advisers employed by education authorities. RE advisers held on better than those of other subjects (thanks in no small part to the statutory nature of SACRE), but when the local authority RE adviser departed they were often not replaced. This left SACRE meetings looking around for the expert guidance they had become used to, and upon which the whole SACRE system now depended. All eyes fell on the diocesan adviser.

Diocesan response

My own experience as a diocesan adviser was that in the short term they became the unpaid local authority adviser – providing national updates, providing advice and dealing with crises when they occurred. Eventually, this arrangement was formalised into a consultancy, either on a freelance basis or through a formal arrangement between the diocese and local authority concerned. The system was falling back on the Church of England once again to became the engine room of the subject. The Church has responded in that principle of 'generous hospitality'. Did this result in a return to the pre-1988 days of confessional RE? There is no evidence that this happened. These now-professional diocesan advisers followed the same national guidance from the Qualifications and Curriculum Authority (QCA 2004) and, when that was closed, from the Religious Education Council (REC) as their remaining local authority colleagues. They produced or managed Agreed Syllabuses that reflected the latest thinking and embedded enquiry-led learning in exactly the same way as their surviving local authority colleagues. These syllabuses covered the same range of religions and, in many cases, were the syllabuses that first introduced the study of Humanism to the RE classroom. By now many of the chairs of SACRE were often faith community representatives willing to give their time without payment. Faith group involvement in RE was far from being problematic, indeed it was proving to be its salvation.

In the autumn of 2016 the Church of England surveyed its diocesan RE advisers about their engagement with RE at SACRE level in preparation for giving evidence at the REC's Commission on Religious Education of that year. Thirty-eight dioceses maintain education teams that include someone with an RE brief; thirty-five of these diocesan advisers responded (a 92% return, which makes it a substantial poll). The results show the extent to which the Church of England has not only become the major player at SACRE level but also could be said to be increasingly maintaining the system across great swathes of the country. A third of SACREs that were reported on had no specialist RE support. On at least 40 percent of the remaining SACREs the diocesan adviser, in one way or another, was providing the formal professional support on RE. On two-thirds the diocesan role was considered 'significant' or more. Diocesan advisers were variously seen as the 'lynch pins' and 'workhorses' of SACREs. The role varied among the SACREs but as one diocesan adviser put it: 'Nothing happens unless I suggest or organise it.' The extent to which diocesan advisers underpin the system is shown by this response from one diocesan adviser working in an urban context:

> I am bought in by eight (perhaps soon to be nine) LAs in (the area) as the Adviser supporting their SACREs with all that entails including agreed syllabus revision, but also handling determinations etc. I am also employed to run termly Primary RE Coordinator Meetings for some of those LAs.

Here is a more typical response showing the extent to which the day-to-day work of SACRE is defaulting to the diocese:

I don't have a main SACRE. In three, I am the adviser; on the 4th I am co-opted. In three of the four SACREs. I run the training for teachers on a termly basis. I liaise between SACRE and NASACRE [National Association of SACREs] and disseminate much of the latest thinking on RE, as well as producing the termly newsletter. I usually attend NASACRE on behalf of at least one of the SACREs. I have been instrumental in producing action plans for two of the SACREs and setting the agenda for meetings. I am also involved in liaising with unions, faith groups and area deans to fill many of the vacancies that occur. I have organised special training events, liaised with the LA and liaised with the Muslim community to produce Ramadan advice for schools. I am also responsible for writing the annual reports for two of the SACREs.

The role of the diocesan RE adviser has never been so central to the continuation of the SACRE system. Without a diocesan adviser bringing their professional expertise many SACREs would not be able to carry out the functions expected of them.

A National Curriculum

Meanwhile, significant concerns were being raised about how effective this delivery of RE was in the classroom. The Ofsted RE report (2010) identified several concerns, around what was the core purpose of the subject, around how attainment was defined and how key concepts and questions were used. Alarm bells in the Christian faith community were set ringing when the report suggested there was:

Specific weaknesses in the teaching about Christianity, with both primary and secondary schools often not paying sufficient attention to the progressive and systematic investigation of the core beliefs of Christianity. (p.6)

The report used as a subheading 'Christianity: A tale of uncertainty'. The report was highlighting the confusion in aims for the teaching about Christianity and the lack of diversity within Christianity that was represented in RE lessons. This struck home.

The latest (and as it turned out final) Ofsted subject report on RE (2013), suggested things were not getting any better. Only 40 percent of RE lessons in primary schools were considered good or better, and the concern around the teaching of Christianity was still there:

> The 2010 report highlighted the concern that too many pupils were leaving school with a very limited understanding of Christianity. Many of the schools visited for the previous report 'did not pay sufficient attention to the progressive and systematic investigation of the core beliefs of Christianity'. The development of this understanding remains one of the weakest aspects of achievement. The current survey included a specific focus on the teaching of Christianity in 30 of the primary schools inspected, and the evidence suggests this is still a major concern. Inspectors judged pupils' knowledge and understanding of Christianity to be good or outstanding in only five of the schools. It was judged to be inadequate in 10 of them, making teaching about Christianity one of the weakest aspects of RE provision. (p.9)

Making the Difference? A Review of Religious Education in Church of England Schools (Church of England Archbishops' Council 2014) found a similar pattern in church schools. It had concluded that something was now needed to raise the quality of teaching and learning in RE about Christianity. This could no longer be left to the struggling locally Agreed Syllabus system. There was now overwhelming evidence that church schools were not fulfilling that original commission from Joshua Watson. The need to return to a systematic and progressive study of Christianity became central policy for the Church of England Education Office.

As the slow fragmentation of the SACRE system began to bite, many began to consider whether the local system was sustainable. The year 2015 saw the publication of three reports all in their own way calling for a more centralised curriculum for RE. Charles Clarke and Linda Woodhead (2015) argue:

> The Religious Education syllabus in county and voluntary controlled schools should no longer be set by a system of agreed syllabuses, but by an agreed national syllabus which would have similar legal status to the requirements of other subjects in the national curriculum. (p.64)

This was also called for in the other reports of that year: Dinham and Shaw (2015) and the Commission on Religious and Belief in British Public Life (2015). In such a climate it was becoming obvious to those in faith communities that throwing time and resources at the local rather than national level was increasingly ineffective.

In 2016 the Church of England launched 'Understanding Christianity' – a resource that takes a systematic approach to the study of Christianity following a spiral curriculum of core Christian concepts. This was in sharp contrast to the more thematic 'Big Questions' approach that had dominated the locally Agreed Syllabuses. It sought to address the issues RE was being criticised for, including the lack of academic rigour, poor teaching and learning and, above all, the confused purpose of the teaching of Christianity. Being rooted in the best practice of RE over the last decade, such a resource was not new in style or approach, but its scope and scale could prove game-changing. It is not the bitty 'additionality' of the diocesan supplemental resources for an Agreed Syllabus. It cannot be introduced in a workshop at a conference, but instead requires schools to commit to 15 hours of training. It is not limited to church schools in a way that a diocesan syllabus might be; instead, being authored by *RE Today* writers, it is geared equally to the needs of community schools in their teaching of Christianity. It reclaims a significant proportion of RE curriculum time to provide a national solution to address the national concerns raised by Ofsted about the teaching of Christianity.

This same year also saw the Board of Deputies of British Jews launch *Judaism GCSE Religious Studies: The Definitive Resource* (Lawton 2016), produced in response to the new GCSE examination specifications, and being in no small measure a response to a perception of years of being misrepresented in the classroom and GCSE exam papers. This resource is a new way in which a faith community is taking back control over what is taught and not taught about them in the classroom. The recent enhancement of the BHA's *Understanding Humanism* website shows they too are committed to this national approach.

It is perhaps not surprising that the Church of England, the Board of Deputies and the British Humanist Association have been first to take such action. They are, or believe they are, the natural authoritative voice in education for those communities. The faith communities that lack such a leading body may find this national approach more problematic.

The developing approach characterised by these new resources from faith and non-faith communities is not without problems. In the limited available curriculum time, which religions and beliefs will be selected for study, and how? If the focus is only on a systematic study of a few selected religions, this will miss much of what RE is, or at least what it has become. There will be little time for the more generic cross-religion themes that have formed so much of the current RE experience, and there will be less scope for the philosophical and ethical questions that have enhanced the subject in recent years. It will, therefore, not produce a rounded religious literacy, but there is a danger of a 'Trivial Pursuit' form of religious literacy. There is something in this argument and it is not the type of RE that the Church of England is seeking. In *Religious Education in Church Schools: Statement of Entitlement* (Church of England Education Office 2016a) three strands to RE were identified:

- To enable pupils to know about and understand Christianity as a living faith that influences the lives of people worldwide and as the religion that has most shaped British culture and heritage.

- To enable pupils to know about and understand other major world religions and worldviews, and their impact on society, culture and the wider word; and to enable pupils to express ideas and insights.

- To contribute to the development of pupils' own spiritual/philosophical convictions.

This combination of the broadly theological, the broadly sociological and the broadly philosophical gives a balanced education in religion that will produce the religiously literate student.

A national RE?

So, there are some trends developing here. As RE becomes increasingly a national subject dealing with national concerns, both societal and educational, then the level of engagement of faith communities (and non-religious worldviews) will be national. Resourcing the teaching of RE is shifting. No longer is time spent producing resources designed to meet the needs of a unit in an Agreed Syllabus mediated via a SACRE. Instead, the picture is now of the development of websites and resources appealing over the heads of the SACRE or examination boards directly to the teachers in the classroom. This is still a 'generous hospitality', but it is now being directed differently. In this time of systems change – with dioceses and faith communities increasingly left leading local RE, and with faith communities (and non-religious worldviews such as the BHA) increasingly being active at national level – this does bring us to the dilemma at the heart of contemporary RE, a dilemma that no other subject really wrestles with: Who owns RE and who decides what should be taught in RE? In History, for example, we teach about people and groups who are rarely around to have a say. A notable historian will codify what pupils need to learn about key topics. For example, for the Second World War the motives of the politicians, soldiers and the people of the day will be analysed based on the evidence. You might even invite into the classroom an old soldier or evacuee, but that is the extent of their voice. In RE, however, a real living thing is under study. Can we do the same in RE? Can a notable RE expert codify what should be taught about a religion often to the children of that religion? Should religious leaders have a say in the content of what is taught about them, or is their role to be invited into the classroom for interview and research, as evidence to be sifted? Are they educators or 'living evidence'?

Perhaps an analogy with performing arts is more helpful. Contemporary art is examined for its structure, its production. The ideas that it is trying to put across are considered, the effectiveness of performance looked at; maybe even the language or symbolism involved are discussed. It is then critiqued and analysed. But the reason that this analysis is done is so that the pupils take part and produce their own art and performance or act out the work of the great authors. When we are dealing with religion, belief and faith, can that be replicated without it becoming too confessional? Would it be appropriate to have a form of religious performance in the classroom? The RE community has never successfully worked this out. Until this question is addressed, the debate about the purpose of RE and the question of who owns RE will remain. RE is unique, and the faith communities must be full partners in RE. They are more than an evidence base or a visiting performance group.

RE in England and Wales since 1944 has been a partnership between faith communities, the local authorities and teachers. It was the very embodiment of what I have suggested is generous hospitality. Even more so today, as the influence of local authorities diminishes, it must make every effort to remain this way. The 1970s and 1980s saw reforms that swung the RE pendulum away from the systematic study of religion to a more sociological and phenomenological approach; it is now, perhaps, swinging back. However, it should not go too far. Post-1944 there was just one religious tradition to study systematically; today there are at least six, plus non-religious worldviews. This will present challenges. A balanced RE curriculum is now needed. It must combine elements of the systematic study or theology clearly needed to give pupils a real knowledge and understanding of the traditions studied. This must be combined with elements of the sociological and phenomenological to help pupils make sense of the religious landscape of the world they will live in. Add into that some of the philosophy and the ethics that has so caught the imagination of pupils over the past few years and we will be approaching the academic, challenging and engaging RE curriculum that is RE at its best. The faith communities must be a central part of this development, but recognising that religious groups and (non-religious groups) are not the only voices in this discussion. To make this work all partners must enter in with that generous hospitality. In doing this we will be promoting a genuine 'religious instruction' in knowledge and understanding that will cheer the spirit of Joshua Watson.

References

Church of England Archbishops' Council (2014) *Making a Difference? A Review of Religious Education in Church of England Schools*. London: Church House Publishing.

Church of England Education Office (2016a) *Religious Education in Church Schools: A Statement of Entitlement*. Accessed on 3 June 2017 at www.churchofengland. org/media/1384868/re_statement_of_entitlement_2016.pdf

Church of England Education Office (2016b) *Vision for Education: Deeply Christian, Serving the Common Good*. Accessed on 3 June 2017 at www.churchofengland. org/media/2532839/ce-education-vision-web-final.pdf

Clarke, C. and Woodhead, L. (2015) *A New Settlement: Religion and Belief in Schools*. Lancaster University: Westminster Faith Debates. Accessed on 25 May 2017 at http://faithdebates.org.uk/wp-content/uploads/2015/06/A-New-Settlement-for-Religion-and-Belief-in-schools.pdf

Commission on Religion and Belief in British Public Life (2015) *Living with Difference: Community, Diversity and the Common Good*. Accessed on 25 May 2017 at www.woolf.cam.ac.uk/uploads/LivingwithDifference.pdf

Dinham, A. and Shaw M. (2015) *RE for REal: The Future of Teaching and Learning about Religion and Belief*. Accessed on 29 May 2017 via http://research.gold. ac.uk/19628

Gay, J. (2016) 'The Training of RE Teachers and the Role of Church College Trusts in Supporting Them.' In B. Gates (ed.) *Religion and Nationhood: Insider and Outsider Perspectives on Religious Education in England*. Tübingen: Mohr Siebeck.

Holloway, V., Dodds, P., Burns, P. and Polley, I. (2014) *Festival Matters: Teaching to Promote Progression and Understanding in Key Christian Festivals*. Salisbury: Diocese of Salisbury Publishers.

Lawton, C. (2016) *Judaism GCSE Religious Studies: The Definitive Resource*. London: Board of Deputies of British Jews.

Ofsted (2010) *Transforming Religious Education*. London: Ofsted.

Ofsted (2013) *Religious Education: Realising the Potential*. Accessed on 25 May 2017 at www.gov.uk/government/publications/religious-education-realising-the-potential

Qualifications and Curriculum Authority (2004) *Religious Education: A non-statutory national framework*. London: QCA.

Chapter 14

DOES RESEARCH MATTER IN THE RELIGIOUS EDUCATION CLASSROOM?

DAWN COX

Research in religious education is as diverse and complex as the subject itself. Amongst all the responsibilities that a classroom teacher must fulfil, what role might research play? This chapter will look at the types of research that may be relevant to religious education teachers, how practitioners might be informed by research and, finally, how they might be involved in research themselves. A small-scale, informal survey of 186 colleagues (completed in October/ November 2016) involved in the discipline of religious education will provide some insight into views and opinions on the role of research throughout the chapter. The survey asked respondents questions about how research was used in their training, any following engagement with research and lastly its place in their current role within religious education. It sought to differentiate between engagement with general pedagogical research and specific religious education research. Finally, it asked respondents to identify their perceived benefits and issues with research in religious education.

What is research in religious education?

For the purposes of this chapter, I propose four possible categories of published academic research that religious education practitioners may consider:

- *General education research*, which focuses on teaching and learning, pedagogy, leadership, ethos or teacher identity, among other topics.

- *Religious education research*, which has a focus on religious education as a discrete curriculum subject. Within this category are further subcategories: distinctive types of religious education in faith or community schools, and in supplementary education environments sponsored by faith communities; religious education around the world; and religious education in England and Wales.

- *Religion research*, which focuses specifically on religious texts, beliefs, practices, ethical issues or inter-religious dialogue, among others.

- *Cross-disciplinary research*, which may move between such disciplines as theology, philosophy, sociology, history, anthropology and psychology.

Much religious education research is international, and this can create a barrier to applicability. The way that religious education is organised and delivered in England and Wales is unique. Features such as locally Agreed Syllabuses, Standing Advisory Councils on Religious Education (SACREs), the nature of religious education in faith as distinct from community schools, compulsory religious education until 19, and the right of parents to withdraw their children are not replicated in other countries. Research that is not based on this system will have limited salience for practitioners in England and Wales.

Whilst such a variety of research types might seem attractive, it may also cause confusion and even conflict in terms of interpreting research and its application into classroom practice. How should a teacher decide which to prioritise? Are the amount and wide-ranging variety of sources more of a hindrance than a help to a teacher who wishes to engage with research? Who decides which should most influence religious education teaching?

Using research

I wish to argue that there are three possible levels of teacher involvement in research. Each has implications in terms of time-commitment, accessibility and possible financial cost. An evidence-*engaged* level of involvement in research demands the reading of full research papers and interpreting their use for the classroom. Evidence-engaged practitioners will understand academic research methodology. An evidence-*informed* level involves reading abstracts or summaries of research, possibly summarised by a third party, and interpreting their use for the classroom. An evidence-*based* level entails using teaching strategies and pedagogies recommended by others, based on research findings. Evidence-based practice means that the practitioner may not know the specific research for the strategy, but relies on its findings being applied to strategies by a third party. I weigh up these approaches, using the measures of time, accessibility and applicability.

Time

Evidence-engaged research is the deepest, most complex and therefore the most time-costly form of teacher involvement. Few respondents in the survey felt they had the time to read academic research. One survey respondent commented explicitly on the 'limited time in which to comb through current research'. The use of the phrase 'combing through' is significant in terms of applicability, discussed below. Most teachers' non-contact time is spent planning and marking. Unless their school has a specific research focus, continuing professional development (CPD) will be determined by other factors, such as the school or subject development plans.

Evidence-informed practice can be much less time-consuming. For example, reading a limited range of abstracts takes the teacher rapidly and directly to the main findings and conclusions. However, what is sacrificed here is a careful regard for how the researcher arrived at the conclusions: the methodologies chosen, the hypotheses and assumptions, the unanswered questions. It may be argued that a general classroom teacher does not need to know and understand the processes behind research papers, so reading summaries may be sufficient. But there are ethical and pedagogical risks involved in digesting research outputs without much attention to their sources. There are other issues with the evidence-informed approach. First, it still requires a teacher to find the abstracts or summaries. This is becoming easier, via websites such as that of the Education Endowment Fund, which is publishing meta-analyses that pull together large sets of research data to provide broad findings for teachers. Second, this still requires the teacher to apply the research to their classroom practice. This may not be simple and, furthermore, not all research will be appropriate.

Evidence-based practice is the least time-consuming for a teacher. Where research output has already been translated into a form that might be applicable in classrooms, the teacher's time spent on searches, reading and checking is reduced. Teachers may even assume that there is no need to read any papers or summaries. However, this approach also has issues. It relies on an intermediary who has read and interpreted the research, and demands a trust in the accuracy and the appropriateness of their recommendations. Most qualitative research findings are nuanced, their messages complex, their recommendations guarded and qualified. Contexts vary: the seductiveness of the phrase 'what works' masks the reality that one classroom is not all classrooms. The further the distance between the teacher and the source, the greater the possibility that these complexities are erased in the well-intentioned belief that this serves accessibility. Finally, evidence-based practice can lead to a 'tips and tricks' teaching method, whereby lessons are reduced to a series of activities that were originally based on research but have become so adapted by teachers that they end up lacking the initial rigour.

Accessibility

Much university-based published research output is behind registration walls, and most refereed journal output is behind a paywall. Unless teachers have access via their school, as alumni or through a teaching association, they face an immediate barrier to research engagement. Just under 25 percent of survey respondents had free access to research papers; some of the respondents work in universities and so will have automatic access. Few teachers or schools would wish to justify the cost of accessing papers with only possible limited benefits to their practice. A subscription to a journal, such as the *British Journal of Religious Education* (*BJRE*), is available on a personal basis as part of National Association of Teachers of Religious Education (NATRE) membership. It also comes with online access through a Chartered College of Teaching subscription. However, the survey shows that the majority of respondents who do have access to the journal only flick through it to see if there is anything of interest. Only 3 percent of respondents said they read 100 percent of the content. Whilst respondents did not give further details on why this is the case, we can infer from their statements later in the survey that it is either due to time limitation, interest in specific articles only or a perception that many articles lack application to their own working context.

RE Today, a termly religious education magazine that forms part of the NATRE membership offer, has a dedicated research section entitled 'Professional Reflection' (previously known as 'REsource'). Its purpose is to provide a resource for teachers of RE that sits between the *British Journal of Religious Education* and *RE Today's* teacher magazine. For a classroom practitioner, it is the link between academic, peer-reviewed research and more practical, classroom-based lesson ideas. It aims to make RE-related research available to teachers in an accessible and useful form, so that they may integrate it into their practice. 'Professional Reflection' aims to include several aspects linked to research, including research posters that give a brief overview of completed research papers and a feature on current research.

This is a practical way for subscribers to gain some access in a manageable way. As an intermediary, it has potential as an important source, helping teachers to be evidence-informed.

Applicability

Some respondents to the survey were also concerned that published research is not easily applied to the classroom, and therefore that the time spent filtering through the research may not be worth the effort. Quality and relevance are frequently cited as potential barriers to using research, as one respondent explained: 'Research often lacks applicability into a variety of contexts.' This highlights the importance of research being easily transferable from research paper to classroom practice. Many teachers want something they can use in their classroom, tomorrow. In the words of another respondent: 'Getting hold of useful, substantiated, relevant and classroom-oriented material that we can make our own is important.' The Religious Education Council states:

> Published research projects into RE-specific learning methods and pedagogy have been influential... Many teachers make eclectic use of these learning methods, often driven by the desire to make RE lively or relevant. (RE Council 2013, p.58)

This seems to suggest that teachers are engaging with religious education research, albeit with a focus on what might be of use in their own classroom. Their use of research might be more determined by the attempt to make their religious education lessons 'lively' or 'relevant', above a true engagement with the process and applicability of the research in their own classroom. The small-scale survey for this chapter shows that more respondents apply general educational research to classroom practice (86.6%) compared to specifically RE research (67.2%). Does this matter? What might be the cause of this difference? How influential really is RE research in the wider teacher population? This is where education blogs can be useful.

Blog series can provide a quick way to engage with research regularly without having to read all the research papers. Bloggers who are serving teachers can serve their teaching colleagues by prioritising messages about applicability. They may reference appropriate research and interpret key findings; crucially, they will often use practical classroom examples to exemplify its applicability. Examples of regular bloggers who have influenced my classroom practice by summarising education research include Alex Quigley (The Confident Teacher) and David Didau (The Learning Spy).

Completing research

Respondents' comments in the survey tended to interpret success in research as that related to teacher involvement. Where research is led and shaped by an external institution, such as a university, the Department for Education or a charitable trust, there is little ownership by the teachers themselves, even if they and their classrooms are the focus. Institution-led research is usually published in journals or on institution websites. It is peer-reviewed and informed by previous research through a literature review, which are an essential part of the process.

Teacher-led research may use the same academic methodologies, but the ownership and authorship is the teacher's. This type of research is frequently done as part of a qualification such as an MA or EdD and may often include action research. Teacher-led research may not be shared beyond its participants, unless it is published with due protection of identities. It will require reading around the issue, including prior research in the area, and will often include classroom trials that teachers do within their own teaching. These may include any trial of a new classroom strategy, which is evaluated for its effectiveness without any process or written outcome. Most teachers will decide whether the strategy has worked, and will either re-use it, adapt it, or reject it. Such classroom trials are usually not shared with anyone else, apart from a limited group such as school colleagues.

If reading research is a time issue for teachers, then completing research will not be any more practical. According to the survey findings, whilst under 50 percent of respondents said they have been involved formally or informally with university-based research, 96 percent do complete classroom trials. Most teacher training courses will involve some form of teacher-led research; but after their initial training, teachers generally lack the time and resources to continue, unless they complete a further qualification or their school is in some way research-engaged. This suggests that teachers are aware that trialling and adapting teaching strategies are useful, and that the quickest way of doing this is by themselves in their classroom.

The principal criticism laid at the door of educational research is the limited relationship between academic, institution-led research and classroom practitioners. This can also lead to generalisations that research is not focused on what teachers need, or that it lacks application to the 'real-life' issues that an RE practitioner faces. However, nationally, there are programmes that are beginning to involve teachers and academic researchers in a more collaborative relationship.

In a non-religious education context, a hybrid of 'institution-led' and 'teacher-led' research has resulted in the development of the Research Schools Network, which shows how it is possible for schools to be involved in educational research at an academic level. This development is working on a model that involves the Education Endowment Foundation and the Institute for Effective Education. It is creating a network of schools that are committed to using and generating research in education. It has significant funding to ensure that schools and their teachers can commit to the time it involves, and is increasing the number of research schools at the time of writing. This might be a model for religious education specialists.

Another important collaboration comes via the ResearchED movement. It provides the opportunity for dialogue between classroom practitioners and academic researchers who are engaged in relevant research. On its website it describes itself as:

> A grass-roots, teacher-led organisation aimed at improving research literacy in the educational communities, dismantling myths in education, getting the best research where it is needed most, and providing a platform for educators, academics, and all other parties to meet and discuss what does and doesn't work.

Those involved work through regional, national and international conferences, usually on a Saturday, and at a very reasonable cost to delegates. Recently, there have been subject-specific events for Mathematics, Science, Modern Foreign Languages and English. Might there be a religious education *RE*searchEd event in the future?

Why religious education research is complex

One survey respondent claimed that religious education research is too often 'researching things that are not tangible or definable'. We might have added 'or clear', in that there is often a confusion and 'lack of clarity' (Religious Education Council 2013, p.30) even over the purpose of the subject. The REC's *Review of Religious Education* acknowledges that '[t]he nature and purpose of RE are not easy to define in straightforward, unequivocal ways' (REC 2013, p.48). It might be argued that several key features of religious education lack a clarity of definition, for example religious literacy, empathy, spirituality and learning from religion (an attainment target widely used in many Agreed Syllabuses). As such, these features are difficult or impossible to measure in quantitative research, and elusive in qualitative analysis. Without collective agreement over the meaning and purpose of religious education, any research on the 'best' approach to teaching the subject will be flawed and contestable.

Further complexity is added by the wide global scope of the subject. For example, in a recent edition of the *BJRE* (2015, Vol. 37, No. 1), only two out of six articles related to British contexts. One discussed Islamic schools, the other addressed spirituality: in both cases, their specificity placed a limit on the extent of their salience. To gain a good general view of religious education research and its applicability, a teacher would have to read the *BJRE* over a sustained period, with the expectation that it would yield some material relevant to their context. However, it should be cautioned that relevance does not mean parochialism. International and cross-sectoral connections can offer insights relevant to religious education in the UK.

Nevertheless, it seems that general teaching research can often seem more applicable. My own research-informed practice has meant more general pedagogy-based classroom trials. Recently I have been particularly interested in cognitive science and how we learn: specifically, how long-term memory has an impact on learning. Amongst others I have read research from Roediger and Karpicke (2006) and Rohrer (2015) that highlighted the importance of spaced practice and interleaving in order to support students in their long-term recall. I have then used these general findings to influence how I have approached curriculum design in terms of interleaved content for the new GCSE. I have also used this reading to continue and develop my use of testing in the classroom, not as a summative measure but for learning itself. I have put low-stakes quizzing into Key Stage 3, and all Key Stage 4 homework is either writing a quiz or completing an online quiz.

In this way, I can see that my reading and exposure to cognitive science research has had an impact on how I teach. It has made my workload more manageable and, more significantly, enabled me to improve students' long-term memory and learning. Nothing has vastly changed in how I teach because of the research, but it has led me to consider what I should be informed by and what I should avoid. Unfortunately, none of this has been based on any research in religious education. This leads me to important yet controversial questions: Is religious education research sufficiently relevant to classrooms? And even if it is, why is religious education research not being used in a similar way to general pedagogical research, as exemplified in my research experience?

The future

The increased use of social media for dialogue and sharing between teachers has made research more prominent and accessible. Online colleagues are sharing links to freely accessed papers, and teachers are sharing blogs in which research evidence is summarised into digestible portions. Institutions and researchers are also becoming more inclined to publish their findings online, without restrictions. Researchers and practitioners too are interacting more frequently via social media. The relationship between teachers and academic researchers seems to be evolving. Whilst this makes for better access, it does little to guarantee quality or reliability. There has been an increase in the number of highly questionable research ideas becoming viral and taking hold of practice, consuming teacher time needlessly (Bennett 2013).

Online teacher forums, such as the *TES* or Facebook groups, show that teachers frequently ask for resources, lesson plans and how to manage workload, rather than for research. The day-to-day pressures of being a teacher will often override the general will to engage with research. Not all survey respondents believe that research in religious education is important; but where it is, they are clear they want practical, relevant research. However, most would also like the time and resources to complete some sort of research themselves. The religious education community needs to address the key obstacles of time, accessibility and applicability. Any solution will need to be practical yet retain academic rigour to be reliable and useful.

Meanwhile, there are current and developing solutions to these that may continue to shape the future of research in religious education.

Time

Farmington Institute Scholarships are available for primary and secondary RE teachers who can make a commitment to research. The scholarship covers a range of costs and, where appropriate, supplies cover for a teacher to be absent from teaching their classes. Scholars are free to investigate any aspect of religious education; however, they are encouraged to focus on issues that have direct value to the teaching of RE in schools, often closely aligned to classroom trials. The expectation is that they present their findings at the annual Farmington Conference and via a written report. These scholarships are attractive in terms of funding and engaging teachers in what will often be their first direct experience of research. Many very distinguished academics began their research with a Farmington Fellowship before progressing to doctoral and postdoctoral studies.

Accessibility

In 2017, a possible bridge between the religious education teaching community and research has been built by the Chartered College of Teaching. It has the goal of being an evidence-led, independent organisation that will support teachers in their use of research. One of their aims is to engage teachers with the latest research on teaching theory and practice to help raise standards across the profession, and raise the quality of debate around school education. Their work will also include developing local networks that collaborate in research between individuals, schools and universities. Additionally, it will provide members free access to published academic papers in a range of journals such as the *BJRE*.

Applicability

Culham St Gabriel's Trust is developing an online knowledge exchange resource to help bridge the gap between institutional, academic research and teachers. The online tool will present research findings in an appropriate format for teachers to be able to apply to classroom practice. Whilst the specifics are not confirmed at the time of writing, it seems an ideal platform for those teachers who can spare a small amount of time reading about topics that may be relevant to their own classroom trials. The applicability of research outputs, whether in education, religion or religious education, will be made clear for a targeted audience. At the same time, teachers will be able to generate searches, ask questions and feed back on the applicability of research. Crucially, this tool will be free. It may well also provide the opportunity for teachers to work alongside researchers on projects that will have direct impact on their classroom practice. This might be the start of a new era of research in religious education.

Conclusion: Does research matter in the RE classroom?

Religious education research matters to teachers, but, at the moment, it probably does not matter enough. It mostly matters when it is relevant and practical. But we should also accept that relevance and practicality can be filters that work negatively as well as positively: they can screen out unlooked-for results and confirm current assumptions and practices. To be evidence-informed or evidence-based, teachers need easier access to more clearly defined messages, whilst avoiding the dangers of crude simplification.

As a minimum, we should expect all religious education teachers to be evidence-based. Some will be evidence-informed, and a probably smaller number can become evidence-engaged, given sufficient experience and stimulus. Progress towards clarifying the proper purpose of the subject, and the scope of its content, would help in focusing research essentials. Social media, more accessible outputs, collaborative conferences and research schools are among the factors helping to bridge the gap. The world of religious education needs to take more advantage of these initiatives.

References

Bennett, T. (2013) *Teacher Proof: Why Research in Education Doesn't Always Mean What It Claims, and What You Can Do about It*. London: Routledge.

Religious Education Council (2013) *A Review of Religious Education in England*. London: RE Council.

Roediger, H.L. and Karpicke, J.D. (2006). 'Test-enhanced learning: Taking memory tests improves long-term retention.' *Psychological Science 17*, 249–255.

Rohrer, D. (2015) 'Student instruction should be distributed over longer periods.' *Educational Psychology 27*, 635–643.

Chapter 15

THE 'DIGITAL TURN'

*What Does RE Teachers' Online
Engagement Mean for RE CPD?*

JAMES ROBSON

Like it or not, teaching is fast becoming a digital profession. In this age of connectivity, modern teachers can draw on a huge array of online resources to support their teaching and wider professional practice. A key part of this online support is social. In the last five to ten years, teachers have been turning to online social spaces, online communities, online networks and online social media in vastly increasing numbers. Discourses from practitioners, policy makers and academics now frequently discuss this kind of activity in terms of continuing professional development (CPD), even suggesting that online networking and peer-to-peer interaction in online social spaces may be the future of CPD (Bloom 2015; Tour 2017). This chapter will explore online engagement and examine its implications for the continuing professional development of RE teachers.

Introduction

RE is an important part of the 'digital turn' (Robson 2016). From the *Times Educational Supplement*'s (*TES*) RE Forum, to Twitter and the Save RE Facebook page, the number of RE teachers interacting with each other in professionally oriented online contexts has grown enormously in the last decade and exponentially in the last five years. For example, in 2011, Save

RE had approximately 800 members; at the end of 2016 it has in excess of 5000 members! This growth in the number of RE teachers interacting with each other in online social spaces is staggering. It raises a number of key questions. Why are teachers interacting online? What in fact takes place within these online social spaces? What are teachers actually getting out of their interactions? Is this the future of continuing professional development (CPD) for RE teachers and, if so, what are the practical implications?

In this relatively emergent field, I'm not convinced an answer to any of these questions is possible at this stage. However, in this chapter I will attempt to discuss the issues around these questions and RE teachers' engagement in online social spaces. In doing so, one of the things I will stress again and again is that *it's complicated*. Despite the large number of positive articles that highlight the benefits of teachers' online interactions for professional learning and CPD (e.g. Bloom 2015; DeNoyelles and Raider-Roth 2016; Tseng and Kuo 2014), social interactions are complex. They come with power relations, structures, hidden meanings, hidden agendas, confusions and misunderstandings. Simply joining Save RE or participating in a chat on Twitter is not necessarily professional learning. Just like the offline world, the messy realities of online social space are complicated!

Background

Although the huge growth in the number of teachers engaging in online social spaces has only happened in the last five to ten years, the idea of online peer-to-peer support networks is not new. In the late 1990s the UK Labour government budgeted over £700 million for the formation of a National Grid for Learning – investing in ICT infrastructure and 'innovative' educational technology. An important part of this spending was on a 'virtual network' and 'virtual teacher centres' (British Education Communications and Technology Agency 1999) that would give teachers access to shared resources and information as well the means to communicate with each other on a local, national and international basis (Department for Education and Employment 1997, p.5). Online tools, communities and spaces were viewed as exciting opportunities for 'teachers to share ideas and good practice, to learn quickly from each other, and find out which schools [were] doing well and why' (quoted in DfEE 1998).

However, although the government built them, the teachers did not come (Selwyn 2000). The virtual teacher centres were quietly dropped a few years later, but the idea of the benefits that online teacher communities could bring to professional practice, and as a means of supporting professional development, has continued in academic and professional discourses. Significantly, though, with few teachers actually engaging in online social spaces for the majority of the first decade of the millennium, these ideas were necessarily expressed mainly in terms of *potential* benefits (Adams 2007; Duncan-Howell 2010; Lock 2006).

What changed was arguably the combination of the rapid growth and dominance of online social media combined with a rapidly changing educational landscape in the UK. Social media now permeates almost every aspect of our lives. It is in the news; it is a key source of news; it is our connection with friends, family and colleagues; it allows us to perform identity; it shapes our identity; it defines our social lives both online and offline; it transforms political structures. In short, social media is a defining aspect of this decade at intra- and interpersonal, local and global levels. At the same time, although in much more mundane terms, the educational landscape in the UK has seen vast upheavals. Academisation and Free Schools, sweeping cuts to local authorities and widespread cuts to CPD budgets have all changed the opportunities available to teachers for continuing their professional development. When combined with the increasing difficulties teachers face in getting time out of school, online peer-to-peer interaction and support are an attractive and cost-effective alternative to traditional models of face-to-face CPD.

As a subject, it is possible RE may be at the extreme end of this trend. Following the sweeping policy reforms of Michael Gove, Secretary of State for Education from 2010 to 2014, many of the traditional support networks for RE teachers have been eroded or simply removed. Face-to-face CPD provision from local authorities is largely a thing of the past; large numbers of RE advisers have been made redundant; academisation and Free Schools have broken up traditional networks of schools and teachers; changes to Initial Teacher Training; and the closure of a number of well-established Postgraduate Certificate in Education courses – these have seen the dissolution of many networks of RE teacher mentors. These changes, when combined with the fact that many RE teachers are the sole subject specialists in their schools (National Association of Teachers of Religious Education 2012), mean that, for many, the only opportunity for subject-specific peer-to-peer interaction is through online social spaces, communities and networks.

What's out there?

In practical terms, there are a number of key online social spaces that RE teachers are using at the moment to engage in professional-oriented peer-to-peer interactions. Just like all online content and spaces, these are likely to change. There are also a number of online social spaces linked with special interest groups within RE, events or locations that I will not list here. However, the largest online social groups, networks and spaces that operate at a national level and bring together teachers of RE from a variety of contexts, schools and career stages are:

- *TES* RE Forum (https://community.tes.com/forums/religious-education.40)

- National Association of Teachers of Religious Education (NATRE) Facebook page (www.facebook.com/NATRE update)

- RE:Online Café (www.reonline.org.uk/forums/forum/caf)

- Save RE[1] Facebook page (www.facebook.com/groups/212329012138235)

- Twitter.

The popularity and use of each of these spaces has waxed and waned over the last five years and will no doubt continue to do so, but at the time of writing, Save RE (with, as already mentioned, membership in excess of 5000) and Twitter dominate in terms of both the number of RE teachers engaging and levels of activity. I will focus on these for the bulk of this chapter.

Save RE was originally established by an RE teacher as a reaction to the policy changes Michael Gove was enacting in the Coalition government. The Academies Bill jeopardised RE's statutory status, while the introduction of the English Baccalaureate (EBacc) was seen as a particularly concerning threat to RE (and still is by many RE professionals), diverting time, resources and teachers away from the subject in favour of priority subjects. Save RE, as the name suggests, was founded as a reaction to these threats. In the first instance, much activity was rooted in sharing letters RE teachers could send to their MPs, voicing concerns about the effects the educational policy changes were having on RE, organising petitions and political activity, commenting on educational news stories and sharing anger. However, as the group has grown, the political focus has been balanced by more practical conversations, requests for resources and sharing of ideas. The name change in 2015 is a reflection of this wider focus.

Twitter is slightly different to Save RE, and indeed all the other online social spaces mentioned above. For these, the online communities within each space are simply those individuals

---

[1] Officially renamed 'Save RE – the Subject Community for RE Professionals' in 2015, but, for ease and in keeping with common practice, will simply be referred to as 'Save RE'.

who have joined the sites. Twitter, on the other hand, offers more agency to users, and places the network-building role in the hands of individuals. A large number of RE teachers now use Twitter, and by following and engaging with particular people, individuals can develop their own networks and build their own support groups. There are also monthly Twitter conversations, based on the hashtag #REchatUK, involving a wide range of RE teachers from across the UK. These are led by NATRE and focus on specific topics or issues.

What are RE teachers actually doing online?

Whether on Twitter, Facebook or another online social space, the question of what RE teachers are actually doing online is complicated. I have written elsewhere that a useful way of conceptualising RE teachers' online engagement is to understand it as taking place across a spectrum of topics, from the very practical and local (related to teachers' own professional practice in their own schools) to the very political and national (related to policy and the identity of the subject at a national level) (Robson 2016, in press). This is, of course, only one way of conceptualising engagement, and within such a spectrum there are different kinds of use (from more passive forms associated with lurking to very active engagement). However, this spectrum provides a useful framework to start discussing some of the wider issues that I think are inherent in professionally oriented online engagement.

Practical learning in a community of practice

In many ways, practical and practice-oriented interaction is the core part of RE teachers' engagement in online social spaces. A huge number of posts on Save RE, for example, revolve around users sharing resources and ideas, other users requesting resources on particular topics, people seeking advice on teaching issues, and teachers looking for help with subject knowledge or professional knowledge (e.g. the advantages and disadvantages of different exam boards). An indicative example would be: 'Does anyone know any useful quotes to use in a lesson on worship in Hinduism?' Hundreds of posts and tweets are made every day requesting and sharing this kind of practical information, and it is clear that a large number of users integrate these peer-sourced ideas, knowledge and advice into their everyday professional practice. For many, this kind of open exchange of resources, advice and knowledge lies at the heart of their online engagement. Here, the online social spaces can be seen as acting as a kind of online community of practice (Lave and Wenger 1991; Wenger 1998), where more experienced teachers can offer practical guidance and advice to less experienced colleagues.

By engaging within such a community, professional wisdom and knowledge can be shared between all users. Individuals have expertise and experience in a variety of different areas and so contribute and learn from others where appropriate. In short, participation in such an online community of practice offers a huge number of opportunities for peer-to-peer professional learning and professional development. However, while this kind of community-of-practice model is often described in the wider literature on teachers' engagement in online social spaces (Trust, Krutka and Paul 2016; Tsiotakis and Jimoyiannis 2016), anyone who has spent any time in contexts like Save RE will be aware that this kind of utopian ideal does not always correspond with the messy realities of online social space. Clearly a great deal of very valuable professional learning and development can and does take place within online social spaces, but a high number of low-quality resources, weak or irrelevant ideas and poor advice are also often shared.

While, it might be argued, that in an effective community of practice, poor ideas and the like should be gently criticised and put right by the more experienced members of the community, this is currently rarely the case, and general constructive criticism online appears to be getting rarer. I suspect there are two main reasons for this. The first is an anti-intellectualist trend that emphasises the need for online social spaces to be 'safe spaces'. While this may have started as a reaction to online behaviours such as trolling and cyber-bullying that take place in other online contexts, in professional online spaces this emphasis appears to be at the expense of critical engagement, critique and debate. A number of instances have occurred where individuals, attempting to discuss the value for teaching and learning of a particular idea or resource, have been criticised and condemned by the wider online community for being too argumentative or critical. Although this may be in tension with the value of criticality many teachers hold dear, at an individual level, in their classrooms and at a community level, this has created a context in which all ideas, knowledge, resources and advice are accepted as valid and beyond critique. Dissenting voices are met with swift and often-intense backlash from the wider community.

The second factor in the lack of critique of poor materials online is the sheer number of teachers now engaging in online social spaces. A community of practice can only operate effectively if the voices of the experts are marked out as such and their advice heard. With membership of online communities for RE teachers now in the thousands it is perhaps inevitable that the more experienced members are hugely outnumbered by less experienced ones. As a result, expert voices are much harder to hear, and high-quality ideas, advice and resources are frequently swamped by more mediocre ones. Without being able to identify expert voices, less experienced users may struggle to distinguish high-quality materials from low-quality materials. They may simply rely on how the community receives resources. Where expert voices are not easily identifiable, crowd-based quality control often leads to a greater tolerance for lower-quality materials, which then, by their community acceptance, are socially validated. This drives the overall quality down and leads to a form of socially validated mediocrity. An example of this can be seen in a post made by a teacher sharing an exercise they had undertaken in a KS4 RE lesson. The teacher had spent time the previous evening filling latex gloves with red jelly, then provided their students with the glove, a board, a large nail and a hammer in order to re-enact the crucifixion. Some individuals on the online social space where this was posted attempted to discuss the underlying pedagogy to this approach and what knowledge students might learn from it. However, their attempts at gentle critique were quickly swamped by dozens of positive comments from other users stating that they were going to do the same thing with their classes. Although I do not want to over-critique this questionable approach here, it is important to note that a less experienced professional coming to the post would see an idea that had been warmly received by a community of RE professionals, and held up as good practice and worthy of use.

Thus, online social spaces can obviously be very effective means of engaging in practical professional learning. However, it is important to ask whether this kind of peer-to-peer interaction always has a positive effect and whether, if not combined with more focused CPD, it will ultimately have a detrimental influence on the RE teaching profession, promoting and socially validating mediocre teaching practice and emphasising the value of 'safe space' at the expense of critical rigour and debate. It is possible that more agentic approaches to online networking, such as that available on Twitter, will be a way of overcoming this issue. Teachers can carefully develop their own professional learning networks made up of experts and those willing to engage in critical debate (Tour 2017). However, it remains to be seen how effective this will be in reality and in the RE context.

Politicking, belonging and taking ownership of RE

Practice-oriented interaction is not the only kind of engagement RE teachers undertake in online social space. As mentioned above, such engagement can be conceptualised as taking place across a spectrum of practical-local and political-national topics. Politically oriented conversations have a huge part to play in

RE-related online social spaces. Teachers share and discuss news stories related to policy development, promote political activity, discuss the legal frameworks around the subject, and more broadly discuss the purpose and aims of RE, its future and identity. At its most basic level, this kind of engagement is a core part of staying up to date with emerging news, developments and debates in the RE world – something that many people would consider to be a core part of professional development and professional identity. However, at a higher level, by participating in these kinds of ongoing rich discussions about the wider issues surrounding RE, it is arguable that teachers are participating in a form of collective meaning-making, negotiating subject identity at a grassroots level. At the same time, by tackling big questions about the nature of RE teaching, those teachers who engage in these kinds of online discussions are also undertaking important identity work, both constructing and performing professional identity positions within online networks and communities of peers. Such engagement may be seen as a unique affordance of online social spaces. It is only by bringing RE teachers together in this way that long, sustained and deep discussions about subject and individual identity are possible. This can be seen as a key part of teachers' professional development and learning as, by analysing and debating the identity of RE, they necessarily reflect on who they are as professionals and who they want to be.

Many practitioners and academics often view the benefits of teachers' online engagement and online networking in pragmatic terms, highlighting the sharing of practical knowledge, wisdom and resources as the most important aspect of CPD that takes place within online social spaces. It is certainly the kind of activity that is likely to have the most immediate impact on practice. However, I would argue that this kind of politically oriented, existential engagement is likely to have a much deeper and more profound impact on teaching practice. By engaging in reflective subject identity work, individual teachers can really reflect on the kind of professional identity they have and should aspire to, and this is most likely to lead to rich, long-lasting professional development.

When I was conducting research in this area (Robson 2016; in press), a substantial number of interviewees highlighted this kind of wider, politically oriented identity work as giving them a sense of belonging, unity and empowerment. Although such feeling may be implicit in more practical types of engagement, the richer debates and discussions around the nature and future of the subject appeared to foster deeper relationships and a greater sense of community. This was vital for many of my participants who felt isolated from their subject-specific colleagues, who benefited psychologically from feeling a part of these wider communities, and who viewed online social spaces as facilitating the creation of national networks of RE teachers in a way that was simply not possible with existing offline infrastructure. This sense of belonging to a national community, combined with politically oriented meaning-making and identity work, gave many of the participants I interviewed a sense of grass-roots subject ownership. This sense of ownership was very empowering for many users, who felt they were taking control of their subject and taking a lead on negotiating its future.

In the context of RE, this sense of teacher subject-ownership that engagement in online social spaces affords is important. As a still locally determined subject, the power of SACREs, local advisers, diocesan advisers, local faith groups, etc. has historically been significant. At a national level, representatives of faith communities; the Association of University Lecturers of Religion and Education; the Association of Religious Education Inspectors, Advisers and Consultants; and other groups and charitable trusts with interests in RE, held together under the RE Council, have been the dominant voices. However, although NATRE has a significant and growing voice at this level, it is arguable that online social spaces are providing RE teachers with a platform to disrupt existing structures by bringing teachers together to engage in RE and wider educational politics at a national level.

It is possible to speculate that existing power structures in the RE world may evolve, partially in relation to policy development and wider educational climate change, but also partially as a reaction to the growing voice of teachers of RE and the challenge to incorporate greater teacher representation in national debates and decision-making in the RE world. This has been a cause taken up and emphasised by NATRE in recent years, and it is arguable that online social spaces have provided an opportunity for an otherwise disparate group of professionals to come together and make their voices heard in a much more coherent and unified way than has been previously possible. Digital technologies' ability to disrupt existing bureaucratic and power-based structures may prove to be a key part of RE teachers' engagement in online social spaces.

Conclusion

RE teachers' online networking and engagement in online social spaces is frequently held up as an important part of professional development. I suspect as financial pressures continue and other forms of CPD for RE teachers get squeezed, many senior leaders and teachers themselves will view subject-specific online peer-to-peer interactions as a core part of professional development. However, as I have attempted to argue throughout this chapter, what actually takes place in professional-oriented online social spaces is complicated, messy and not always beneficial. Teachers' online interactions challenge our understanding of what professional development actually means in an increasingly digital world and necessitates a broad conceptualisation that sees CPD both in terms of the sharing of practical wisdom as well as ongoing identity work at both subject and individual level. This can enhance the disruptive nature of technology and provide RE teachers with a greater, more powerful and more cohesive national voice. Engagement in online social spaces can offer RE teachers a new way of being professionals and a new mode of being teachers, and it can be an empowering developmental experience. However, in practical terms, this requires careful navigation and negotiation. As mentioned above, the tyranny of mediocrity and the stifling nature of 'safe space' are constant challenges in this developing field. But, through collaborative negotiation and identity work, RE teachers can develop their own understandings of the subject, of who they are and of who they want to be as professionals. In doing this, RE teachers can approach online social spaces with appropriate criticality and use them to shape their professional development in an agentic and empowering way.

References

Adams, J. (2007) 'Artists Becoming Teachers: Expressions of Identity Transformation in a Virtual Forum.' *International Journal of Art & Design Education 26*, 3, 264–273.

Bloom, A. (2015, May) 'Why Twitter could hold the secret to better #CPD.' *Times Educational Supplement*, p.8.

British Education Communications and Technology Agency (1999) *Making the Most of the National Grid for Learning: An Introduction to the National Grid for Learning*. Coventry: Becta.

DeNoyelles, A. and Raider-Roth, M. (2016) 'Being an "agent provocateur": Utilising online spaces for teacher professional development in virtual simulation games.' *Technology, Pedagogy and Education 25*, 3, 337–353.

Department for Education and Employment (1997) *Connecting the Learning Society*. London: The Stationery Office.

Department for Education and Employment (1998) 'Blunkett announces details of biggest ever investment in schools information and communication technology' [Press release]. London: DfEE.

Duncan-Howell, J. (2010) Teachers making connections: Online communities as a source of professional learning. *British Journal of Educational Technology*, 41(2), 324–340.

Lave, J. and Wenger, E. (1991) *Situated Learning: Legitimate Peripheral Participation*. Cambridge: Cambridge University Press.

Lock, J.V. (2006) 'A new image: Online communities to facilitate teacher professional development.' *Journal of Technology and Teacher Education 14*, 663–678.

National Association of Teachers of Religious Education (2012) *An Analysis of a Survey of Teachers on the Impact of the EBacc on Student Opportunity to Study GCSE RS: A Fourth Survey – July 2012* (V1.1). Accessed on 3 June 2017 at www.retoday.org.uk/media/display/NATRE_EBacc_Survey_2012_Final.pdf

Robson, J. (2016) 'Engagement in structured social space: An investigation of teachers' online peer-to-peer interaction.' *Learning, Media and Technology 41*, 1, 119–139.

Robson, J. (in press) 'Performance, structure and ideal identity: Reconceptualising teachers' engagement in online social spaces.' *British Journal for Educational Technology* [Advance online publication]. doi:10.1111/bjet.12551

Selwyn, N. (2000) 'Creating a "connected" community? Teachers' use of an electronic discussion group.' *Teachers College Record 102*, 4, 750–778.

Tour, E. (2017) 'Teachers' self-initiated professional learning through Personal Learning Networks.' *Teaching, Pedagogy and Education 26*, 2, 179–192.

Trust, T., Krutka, D.G. and Paul, J. (2016) '"Together we are better": Professional learning networks for teachers.' *Computers & Education 102*, 15–34.

Tseng, F.C. and Kuo, F.Y. (2014) 'A study of social participation and knowledge sharing in the teachers' online professional community of practice.' *Computers & Education 72*, 37–47.

Tsiotakis, P. and Jimoyiannis, A. (2016) 'Internet and higher-education critical factors towards analysing teachers' presence in on-line learning communities.' *The Internet and Higher Education 28*, 45–58.

Wenger, E. (1998) *Communities of Practice: Learning, Meaning and Identity*. Cambridge: Cambridge University Press.

POSTSCRIPT

Purposing RE for a Better Future

ZAMEER HUSSAIN

In a recent conference I attended, RE teachers were asked to create a classic 'Diamond 9' on the purpose of RE at Key Stage 3. Nine options were given, from 'preparation for GCSE' to 'developing respect for the subject' to 'developing skills'. The cards kept swapping and moving order as the participants passionately, but politely, disagreed over what should go on top, bottom and in-between. The movement only stopped when the time limit was up; otherwise it could have continued for longer. This is a microcosm of the bigger debate going on between colleagues on what the purpose of RE is. The question arises: If we cannot agree on the purpose of RE, how can we clearly map out a better future for the subject?

At the time of writing, as someone rather new to the profession, it has always confused me as to why this debate is taking place. Do other subjects have heated debates on their general purpose? If so, do those debates divide and weaken them? I presume the core purpose of History is to learn about history, and the core purpose of Geography is to learn about geography. So in RE we should be learning about religion. Yes, we can debate what defines a 'religion' and how religion relates to non-religious worldviews. The range of our content can be open. However, we need to be clear that the principal aim of the subject should be this: learning about religion, as the name suggests. Promoting respect, fostering values, creating space for spirituality, exploring personal meaning – these are all fine things, but they are not RE. When we conflate these things with our subject's aim, we create confusion. How did we allow it to become so complicated?

In addition to this, perhaps RE has been diluted by other areas of the curriculum. Since the exclusion of RE from the EBacc, several secondary schools have reduced the curriculum time for RE. To salvage this lost time, RE departments might offer to teach other disciplines. So now in some places, RE includes several aspects of Citizenship and PSHE. Would another subject do this? If a pupil studies an amalgamated subject at KS3 and then chooses the new GCSE Religious Studies, will they not feel that they have been sold a lie? You cannot blame a young person for rebelling against the GCSE when their RE lessons turn from discussing the Illuminati to studying the Gospel of John. But if the students are given appropriate rigour in RE at KS3, then they will know what to expect at GCSE.

So what is the core purpose of RE? Let us start with what the core purpose of RE is not. RE is not studied to solve extremism and stereotypes. RE is not studied to promote community cohesion and tolerance. RE can help with these, but it is not the aim. The subject should be treated as an academic discipline in its own right. The core purpose of RE should be to give young people religious literacy. Personally, I define religious literacy as being able to converse about religions and worldviews confidently, accurately and wisely. When asked why I love RE, my answer is very simple: RE makes me understand why people believe and do certain things, whether those things are good or bad. Religious literacy gives a person this understanding. This comes from actually studying the worldviews we have on offer.

If the standards of RE are high and it is taught confidently, it will automatically have positive by-products. Excellent RE will allow students to understand what people believe, why they believe it and why they do certain things stemming from these beliefs. If a young person understands this, they will be able to automatically challenge extremism and stereotyping, because they understand where it comes from and what a distortion it is. Community cohesion and tolerance will be achieved because students will appreciate other people's worldviews, having studied them in sufficient depth. Religious literacy in itself is a public good, which can be achieved by treating RE as what it is – learning about religion. Religion, or having a worldview, is a reality and it is important for our young people to engage with it. There is no need to make it 'trendy' just because most religions and worldviews are rooted in the past. If students are expected to read the plays of Shakespeare and poems of Wordsworth, then why are we ashamed to let our students navigate through the Bible or the hymns of the Guru Granth Sahib? There is no better sight than this in the RE classroom.

So what would I like to see in the future? Although it may seem like a utopia, as a teacher I want several things to change.

- The key thing we need is an agreed purpose; and this purpose should be religious literacy. This could come in the form of a National Curriculum for the subject. This may start with a period of rebellion from some people who disagree. But if something concrete is there, it removes the room for confusion. This overarching aim of religious literacy will implicitly cover the other good intentions that people may have.

- I would like to see RE as a subject respected in its own right, without it being underpinned by the ethos of other disciplines, or patronised as a social cohesion project.

- RE should be given an amount of time in the curriculum that is fair, where senior leaders are not pressured to reduce its time in order to prioritise other subjects. In the time we are given, however, we need to make the most of it by prioritising depth over breadth. Our society now has access to so much information, and our young people will not settle for skimming over the surface when we live in a world of asking questions.

- To deliver this, we need many more qualified specialist teachers, and like many RE teachers I want the government to step up on this.

- The right to withdraw from RE should be changed. Do other subjects have to put up with this? It is out of date, and in some ways an insult to our subject.

Changing the name of our subject is a kind of rebranding which has already happened in several schools. Some teachers do it because they want their subject to be more 'appealing' to parents and pupils – not seeing it as a form of useless preaching. Maybe the time will come for a change of name, but at the moment I feel this is a red herring that is distracting RE teachers and policy makers from agreeing on the purpose of RE.

There is no doubt RE is a special subject (but anyone who loves their subject would argue this about their own). RE has the power to benefit the world; this mentality should be kept. There is so much potential for it that needs to be unlocked. It is time to end the marginalisation and belittlement of RE at national level. If we agree a shared purpose, and teach really well what our subject requires us to teach, we will be taken seriously; and the young people we teach, and all of society, will ultimately benefit from the subject.

BIOGRAPHICAL NOTES ON CONTRIBUTORS

Mike Castelli was an RE teacher and head of department for 19 years before becoming an RE adviser and latterly a university RE tutor for 20 years. Mike's research and publications are in the areas of faith schools, an English Islam and teaching RE dialogue. Mike is Executive Chair of the Association of University Lecturers in Religion and Education.

Phil Champain worked for two decades in international peacebuilding before becoming the Director of 3FF, one of the UK's leading interfaith charities. He is also a trustee of Music in Detention, an NGO that provides music workshops for those detained within the UK's Immigration Removal Centres, and is a founder of KitchenRituals, which aims to strengthen relations through the application of food-based rituals.

Mark Chater is a qualified RE teacher. He taught in three schools and three universities before becoming RE's National Adviser with the then Qualifications and Curriculum Authority. Mark is now Director of a charitable trust that supports research, development and innovation in RE. His doctoral thesis concerned the relationship between confessional and non-confessional models of RE in the UK. Mark is co-author of *Does RE have a Future?* (2012, Routledge).

Dawn Cox is an experienced secondary teacher. Her roles have included Advanced Skill Teacher, assistant principal, lead practitioner, Specialist Leader in Education and Head of RE.

She is interested in teaching and learning, specifically in assessment and research in education. She is active on social media and has a popular blog on teaching and leadership in schools.

Gillian Georgiou has taught Religious Education/Studies and Philosophy in state secondary schools and currently works as the RE Adviser for the Diocese of Lincoln. She sits on the RE Development Group at the Church of England Education Office and is a representative of the Archbishops' Council to the RE Council of England and Wales.

Derek Holloway was an RE teacher and head of department working in community schools in Essex and Wiltshire for 17 years. He then became a diocesan and local authority RE adviser for 15 years before taking up his current post with the Church of England Education Office.

Zameer Hussain is a qualified RE teacher and head of department. He received a BA degree in Philosophy from the University of Essex in 2012 and completed his PGCE in Religious Education at King's College London in 2013. He has been a teacher since then and a head of department since 2014. He is co-author of *GCSE Religious Studies Shi'a Islam: Beliefs and Practices* (2017, Al-Khoie Foundation) and will be serving as a member of National Association of Teachers of Religious Education executive from January 2018.

Richard Kueh is a Senior Curriculum Leader in the Inspiration Trust, a multi-academy trust of thirteen schools. He leads on curriculum development, research, CPD and Initial Teacher Training in Religious Education and Philosophy. A qualified RE teacher and former head of department, Richard has shaped his practice in both the state and independent sectors. He wrote his Cambridge doctoral thesis on the philosophy of Hans-Georg Gadamer. Richard has undertaken research into the rationale for Religious Education, supported by a Farmington Fellowship. His diverse interests include philosophical hermeneutics, Biblical exegesis, reception theory and, most recently, the relationship between Philosophy, Religious Studies and Theology as academic disciplines and Religious and Philosophical Education.

Clive A. Lawton has been a teacher, headteacher and local authority deputy director of education. Formerly a chief examiner for A Level Religious Studies in the north of England and a scrutineer for the School Examinations and Assessment Council, Clive has been involved in RE for over 30 years. Over that time, he has trained teachers, lectured on aspects of RE, published several books and advised on the creation of a number of Agreed Syllabuses. Now President of the Shap Working Party for World Religions in Education, he was the sole editor and compiler of its calendar of religious festivals for over a decade and, through that role, has become a pre-eminent calendrical expert. Honoured with an OBE in 2016 for services to education, Clive is now Chief Executive of the Commonwealth Jewish Council. Amongst other qualifications, Clive has a Master's degree in Hinduism and Islam and has been long involved in inter-religious dialogue and trialogue.

Andrew Lewis is an assistant headteacher and Director of Religious Education at St Bonaventure's School in the London Borough of Newham. He has worked at a number of Catholic comprehensive schools in the Diocese of Brentwood, holding both pastoral and subject leadership positions. He has contributed to RE nationally through his work with Culham St Gabriel's, Teach First and the Catholic Education Service. He has been involved in TeachMeet London and ran the London RE Hub in 2015 and 2016. Andrew has spoken at a number of events including Westminster Briefings, various TeachMeets and regional RE training days. He has published a textbook for the new GCSE specification and is involved in a new series of Key Stage 3 textbooks to be published in 2017. He was nominated for *TES* Teacher Blogger of the Year in 2016 and frequently tweets and blogs about RE and wider education.

Neil McKain has been a head of Religious Studies for ten years. He graduated in Theology and RS from the University of Leeds in 2002 and has an MA in Philosophy and Religion from Heythrop College. His Farmington Fellowship project in 2012 centred on the use of formal debating in RE. As well as serving on the National Association of Teachers of Religious Education executive, Neil is a textbook author and an educational adviser for both TrueTube and the British Humanist Association.

Mary Myatt taught RE and Latin in London, Cambridge and Suffolk before becoming the Suffolk RE Adviser and is now an independent school improvement adviser. With Jane Brooke she co-founded the RE Quality Mark which recognises high-quality provision in schools. She writes, speaks at conferences and works with school leaders on the link between school values and outcomes for pupils. Her latest book is *Hopeful Schools* (2016, Mary Myatt Learning, Ltd.).

James Robson has been working in the fields of educational research, educational technology and RE for the last ten years at both Oxford University and a charitable trust that supports research, development and innovation in RE. His doctorate focused on RE teachers' use of social media, and he is currently working on a knowledge exchange intervention supporting collaboration and dialogue between researchers and RE teachers.

Sushma Sahajpal runs Connectar, a creative education consultancy supporting RE teachers with training, resources and specially commissioned whole-school RE enrichment events. An Oxford graduate with expert knowledge of the Dharmic (Indian) traditions, Sushma has provided consultancy for RE syllabus reviews as well as faith expertise for the BBC and other organisations. She has recently been commissioned to write an A Level Hinduism textbook.

Dr Peter Schreiner studied Education, Theology and Social Science at the University of Mainz. He worked for many years at the Comenius-Institut, a 'Protestant Centre for Research and Development of Education' in comparative religious education and intercultural education. Since September 2015 Peter has been the Director of the Institute. His doctoral thesis (Free University of Amsterdam and University of Erlangen-Nürnberg) discussed the Europeanisation of education and the role of religion.

Adam Whitlock is Senior Leader at Ark Burlington Danes Academy with responsibility for the Faculty of Religious Education, the Extended Project Qualification and preventing extremism. He has an interest in developing the critical realist pedagogy, holistic student mentoring, post-16 progression and counter-extremism in schools. He has delivered a keynote speech at the National Association of Teachers of Religious Education's 'Strictly RE' conference, regularly visits the Institute of Education at UCL to lecture RE trainees, and features in the Home Office's national workshop to raise awareness of Prevent.

Kathryn Wright has taught RE in state secondary schools and now works as an independent RE consultant with a range of organisations. She is currently completing a PhD researching the purpose of RE and pedagogy in Church of England schools. She is a qualified Section 48 inspector and assesses schools for the RE Quality Mark. She is a co-opted member of the National Association of Teachers of Religious Education executive and sits on the RE Council of England and Wales.

SUBJECT INDEX

AUTHOR INDEX